ADHD WORKBOOK FOR MEN

ADHD WORKBOOK FOR MEN

EXERCISES AND STRATEGIES TO IMPROVE FOCUS, MOTIVATION, AND CONFIDENCE

Puja Trivedi Parikh, LCSW, BCBA

ROCKRIDGE
PRESS

For general information on our other products and services or to obtain technical support, please contact our Customer Care Department within the United States at (866) 744-2665, or outside the United States at (510) 253-0500.

Rockridge Press publishes its books in a variety of electronic and print formats. Some content that appears in print may not be available in electronic books, and vice versa.

Interior and Cover Designer: Irene Vandervoort
Art Producer: Melissa Malinowsky
Editor: John Makowski
Production Editor: Rachel Taenzler
Production Manager: Holly Haydash

Illustrations © Anugraha Design/Creative Market

Paperback ISBN: 978-1-63878-087-8
eBook ISBN: 978-1-63878-244-5
R0

CONTENTS

INTRODUCTION

If you're reading this, you're a man on a mission to change your life by learning more about how attention-deficit/hyperactivity disorder (ADHD) affects you—and what you can do today to effectively and proactively manage your life.

I'm Puja Trivedi Parikh, a licensed psychotherapist and behavior analyst in private practice. For over a decade, I have worked with adults with ADHD, helping them understand, appreciate, and manage their unique sets of social, emotional, and behavioral challenges. As a clinician, I use a person-centered, strengths-based, holistic, and collaborative approach, with my goal being to empower people to realize their unique strengths, identify their values, and approach the world with clarity and confidence.

Adults with ADHD struggle to identify and acknowledge their strengths and have a harsh inner critic whose default is to say, "You are lazy," "You aren't successful and will never be," or "You can't do this." That is not your own voice—rather, that is what you have learned to believe through your experiences in a world where the ADHD brain is often seen only for its differences, or as a pathology, with no mention of the strengths that come with it. The power of authenticity, passion, and curiosity that comes with you being *you* can—and will—make it possible for you to pursue a life that is aligned with your values, purpose, and intentions. To help you embrace yourself as you are now, I've included exercises that go beyond this workbook's practical advice.

Finally, I want you to know that this workbook and the exercises included in it are written by someone who is walking the walk, not just talking the talk. I was diagnosed with ADHD well into adulthood. Receiving the diagnosis was unexpected yet welcome, because I was able to shift my self-perspective and embrace my neurodivergence as a gift. Overall, I feel I am better at what I do as a clinician as a result of my diagnosis, while really letting go of toxic understanding and appreciating my strengths. I struggle with organization and time management at times; I accept that and continue to work daily on ways to improve in these areas. In writing this book, I feel more empowered in my capacity as a clinician who really understands adult ADHD, lives its pros and cons on a daily basis, and really means it when I say, "I know how you must be feeling."

HOW TO USE THIS WORKBOOK

The workbook's six chapters flow intuitively, as the order of topics might proceed in clinical sessions, but this workbook is not meant to replace medical treatment or advice. If you have any questions regarding your medications or response to treatment, or need specific behavioral support, it is always a good idea to check in with your therapist or doctor. Think of this workbook as a useful complement to your existing treatment plan. You can bring it with you to sessions if you want to review and process something further with your therapist or doctor, and/or you can work on the exercises between sessions to continue your momentum and get the results you are looking for. Harness the power of managing your ADHD and make it work for you—not against you.

Chapters 1 and 2 of this book help you learn more about ADHD and how its symptoms affect men—particularly in terms of career, relationships, emotional regulation, self-esteem, and overall quality of life. In chapters 3 and 4, you'll learn how to debunk ADHD myths and stereotypes, as well as how to form healthy, adaptive habits that stick. Finally, chapters 5 and 6 discuss embracing your neurological differences and challenges as opportunities to grow and learn new skills. They also discuss when to seek professional care for medication management and ways to engage in behavioral therapy with an experienced clinician who specializes in treating ADHD in men. The chapters do not have to be completed in order, so feel free to move around or start where you prefer. For example, if you want to explore whether seeking professional care is best for you sooner rather than later, start with chapter 6.

It may be tempting to rush through the content or exercises (speaking from personal experience), but I highly recommend that you take your time and immerse yourself in the work. I encourage you to regularly schedule time on your calendar for self-awareness, reflection, and growth—aim for progress and practice over perfection. This strategy may feel boring in the short term, but it will help you in the long term, and that is why you have chosen to use this workbook—as a portal into self-growth and change.

If life gets in the way and you need to take a little time off from using the workbook, that's totally fine. You can always come back to it and pick up where you left off. There is no time limit for completing the workbook; the material only works for you if you are present, open, and willing to take a moment for yourself and work toward your desired outcomes. Once you complete the workbook, keep it handy in case you would like a refresher—or you can do the exercises again to confirm your progress and celebrate how far you have come in your journey!

A Note for Trans Men

Thank you for choosing to use this workbook to help you work through your ADHD journey. Please feel warmly welcome here. I strive to achieve an attitude and approach that is open to diversity, inclusion, and different abilities. That said, I may unintentionally omit or misunderstand something pertinent to trans men because of my cisgender experience. But I am always open to learning more and doing better. I am neurodivergent, and when I write or speak, I feel I am speaking for those like me, who have challenges that the majority of people in this world cannot always understand or forgive. I can't wait for you to start using this workbook and I hope you find it helpful.

The content is written from a psychosocial and behavioral perspective, emphasizing my clinically and research-informed perspective that ADHD is a brain-based—*not a gender-based*—disorder where genetics, environment, and social and psychological influences underlie how ADHD is developed and to what degree it can impact someone. That said, the practical information is ready-to-use, and the engaging strategies and exercises in this workbook have been created using a psychosocial approach. They are holistic, use the environment and self as context, and are focused on cultivating a growth mindset, which I believe is important in learning to be flexible so that we can adapt and thrive in any situation (in this case, having the traits of an ADHD mind). For it is said, "Those who learn to bend will never break."

> *I always have a choice, and I choose to go on this journey of self-improvement and growth by doing something differently each day, in order to become better than I was yesterday.*

CHAPTER 1

The Effects of ADHD on Men

In this chapter, we will focus on how the core symptoms of adult ADHD, associated executive functioning skills deficits, and society's expectations of men all impact various aspects of men's lives. Knowing yourself, including your strengths, is an asset in helping you increase your self-esteem and confidence as you figure out how to manage the ADHD symptoms that are preventing you from living your best life.

Core symptoms of adult ADHD include hyperactivity, distractibility, an inconsistent ability to sustain attention, and difficulties with emotional regulation (how we manage and control our emotions). Executive functions are controlled by the frontal lobe of the brain, and are the abilities that help you do the things you do every day. Executive functions include organization and planning, flexibility, time management, self-awareness, attention, emotional regulation, inhibition, and impulse control. For individuals with ADHD, executive functions don't always work the same way as they do for individuals without ADHD, and they require extra effort—for example, through external cues such as calendars, notes, and voice memos—to be used effectively. There are many simple strategies you can use to start doing these things, and this topic is discussed in more detail later in this workbook.

The demands of modern society and societal expectations of men—to be providers, protectors, and leaders, and to be strong (physically and emotionally)—often leave men with ADHD feeling frustrated. If they cannot live up to society's demands and their own (often very high) standards, this can draw out challenging traits associated with ADHD, such as addiction, substance abuse, anxiety, depression, procrastination, underachievement in school or at work, poor organization skills, the inability to start and finish things, cluttered living environments, and indecisiveness. Many people, especially men, also have difficulty expressing their feelings and coping with them effectively. This contributes to the unique challenges that men with ADHD face across all areas of life due to the important roles that self-regulation and emotional regulation play in mood and getting things done. Allow yourself to feel compassion for and acceptance of yourself as you continue with the exercises and content in this chapter.

ANGEL'S STORY

Angel was frequently late getting to work, doctor's appointments, and dinner with friends. He felt rushed, like there was never enough time in the day, like he was always trying to catch up. He frequently stayed up late scrolling through his phone, feeling restless and unable to sleep. Sometimes he had "a few beers to unwind." Angel often missed project deadlines or submitted work he had completed hurriedly, filled with errors that required significant revision. Angel had lost many jobs due to careless mistakes, missed deadlines, and not showing up or clearly communicating with his managers or coworkers about his absences or unavailability. Friendships and other relationships were difficult to maintain because he rarely responded to invitations, reached out to catch up, or took the initiative to organize plans. Angel never felt smart enough or good enough at anything he did in life. He often told himself he would never find a job he liked, a fulfilling romantic relationship, or friends who really understood him.

Work and Commitments

As you read Angel's story, some of his experiences may have resonated with you. Angel's challenges had a lot to do with his executive functioning skills, not his level of intelligence or his abilities. He was able to get jobs but unable to keep them due to his challenges with time management, planning and organization, self-awareness, and emotional regulation. The anxiety and stress we all experience when faced with initiating and completing projects or tasks that require many steps, along with the self-imposed goal of delivering a perfect project, can cause the brain to get overwhelmed and freeze. This can lead us to seek immediate relief or escape from the emotional distress by doing something not stressful, like watching videos or scrolling through social media apps. This is called procrastination. We all engage in it to some extent, and it can be very difficult to overcome.

For adults without ADHD, the key difference is that the executive functioning skills work as intended (at least, more often than not), allowing the individual to plan, organize, focus, and manage their discomfort and dislike of the task long enough to complete it. Now, this does not mean that the task is completed exceptionally well, without any room for improvement. It is just that the individual without ADHD is able to complete the task unimpeded. For such an individual, it is easier to just get the task done and move on, like paying a bill and throwing out the paperwork right away, instead of letting bills pile up, leading to clutter and getting charged late fees if payments are submitted past their due dates.

With the societal expectations for men to be strong and to act as providers, income and status are deeply tied to men's ideas of success and self-esteem in personal and professional social circles. The stress, feelings of shame, and guilt from procrastinating and then rushing to complete a task may lead to frequent and/or critical errors that can lead to being fired. Men with ADHD often have employment gaps they need to explain, are underemployed, or struggle with underachievement due to fear of failure, which can make the ADHD brain stuck and indecisive. Due to these circumstances, the paralyzing anxiety and depression that men with ADHD may experience puts them at high risk for car accidents; self-medication with nicotine, alcohol, or drugs; addiction; divorce or separation from a partner; avoidance of social interactions due to feelings of low self-esteem caused by comparing their life to the successful lives of others; an inability to feel they are good enough; and a feeling that everything is their fault. These struggles suppress the reality that men with ADHD are smart, ambitious, personable, and creative, with an intuitive style that allows them to provide unique insights.

Check Yourself Checklist

Use this exercise to write down information that will help you focus your attention on the things you would like to improve upon in the work and commitment areas of your life impacted by ADHD. Expanding your self-awareness can help you get clarity about what you want to accomplish, why you want to do it, and how to get there.

List three things you think you are not so good at.

1. ....

2. ....

3. ....

THEN: The following is a list of skills. Which skills get in the way of the three things you listed in the previous section as things you feel you are not so good at? Using a rating scale of 1 to 5, with 1 being "not a problem at all" and 5 being "a significant problem," rate each skill.

_____ Organization		_____ Initiative
_____ Planning		_____ Time management
_____ Adaptive/flexible thinking		_____ Self-awareness/self-direction of attention
_____ Memory recall		
_____ Impulse control		_____ Prioritizing task by urgency, not preference
_____ Emotional regulation		

NEXT: Circle the three or four skills you gave a high rating to and that you want to work on improving.

LAST: Write down three detailed action goals that describe how you will work toward improving these skills.

1. ....

2. ....

3. ....

Family and Relationships

Friendships with individuals who have ADHD can feel like a one-way street. Most people have friends they enjoy getting together with and find easy to connect with. But if one person is putting in way more effort to stay connected, resentment or indifference can develop due to the imbalance, and the friendship can start to feel like a chore. Impulsive behavior—such as saying something insensitive and not realizing it, or blurting out a secret that was meant to stay between friends—is one of the factors that makes sustaining friendships difficult for individuals with ADHD. Staying socially connected and planning regular social interactions is important for your overall well-being. If you are struggling in this area, take a minute to regroup and have an authentic conversation with friends that you want to keep in your life and see if they can help you.

Men with ADHD often become overwhelmed and appear detached or emotionally withdrawn in relationships, leading to conflict, seeking other relationships that are fulfilling, or becoming hyperfocused on work or other projects, thus not giving their partner and relationship attention. Additionally, the need for novelty can make sex with one partner boring. The yearning for new experiences can be strong at times, leading to affairs and thrill-seeking behaviors that can boost the reward system in the brain. Sex can also be used as an escape from feelings of boredom because of the chemicals that the brain gets as a result of sexual contact and release. For some, sex can also become an addiction, making it hard to sustain a marriage. Infidelity, separation, divorce, high conflict levels, and trust issues are common concerns that can surface. Conflict surrounding the division of household chores and tasks can arise, with partners becoming resentful if they are always stuck with being in charge of paying the bills on time and managing the finances, including monitoring spending. Such a situation can create a parent–child dynamic between a couple.

Parenting can be stressful, erratic, and inconsistent, especially if you are parenting a child who also has ADHD. Establishing schedules, routines, and healthy boundaries can be hard. Caregiving can become boring due to the nature of the repetitive and routine tasks associated with it. It can feel daunting to manage multiple schedules, coordinate pickups and drop-offs, and have lunch and other meals ready, while also making sure your work is done, you eat, you shower . . . and so on. You may also become frustrated that your child does not comply with requests, leading to a power struggle or yelling to get things done. This creates a stressful environment for everyone, including you. Use the skills you are good at and work together with your partner to set up a system that works for your family.

Figuring Out What Really Matters

The following exercise is designed to help you examine the relationships in your life and identify the areas where you would like to see improvement. There are no right or wrong answers here—only what helps you is important. In the space provided and/or in a separate journal, write how you plan to improve the quality of your relationships, then schedule a time and date to get started.

Here are some prompts to help you get going:

1. What do I want to put into my relationships?

2. Which relationships are important for me to prioritize?

3. What do I want my loved ones to think or feel about me?

4. What actions do I need to take to show my love and support?

5. What barriers do I need to overcome to address chronic issues in my relationships?

6. How can I use my strengths to develop the skills I need?

Time Management

Difficulty with time management is a very common and challenging issue related to ADHD. Time management and organizational abilities are two significant executive functions to work on because they affect all aspects of your life. Challenges include not scheduling yourself enough time to get to and from places, as well as underestimating task completion times, leading to procrastination, missing deadlines, or turning in work at the very last minute, often work that has many errors and does not reflect your true capabilities.

Angel's story earlier highlighted many examples that reflect the way time management issues can show up. ADHD often comes with an absent internal sense of time. You may have heard it referred to as "time blindness," where the concept of time is lost on individuals with ADHD, leading to poor scheduling, doing something for one hour but thinking it has only been 20 minutes, or not setting realistic expectations regarding time commitments. Some common challenges include:

- Being chronically late for work, school, or personal events

- Having a hard time starting projects that require multiple steps

- Difficulty prioritizing tasks and often choosing to do a less urgent task first

- Taking longer to complete tasks than others who don't have ADHD

- Procrastination, or avoiding something because of the effort it involves, a lack of interest in the task, or not knowing where to start or how to do it

- Focusing on perfection at the expense of overall progress toward a goal, leading to projects being abandoned midway

- Experiencing feelings of guilt, depression, anxiety, shame, anger, and frustration after repeatedly being unable to maintain schedules and timeliness

Time Is of the Essence

Time management can be difficult for people with ADHD due to time blindness, or an incorrect perception of time and the effort required to complete tasks. Some tasks take more time and effort than others, and this is not a reflection of your intelligence or skills. Focus on your goals, cultivating the skills required to achieve them, and celebrate your progress. Begin by comparing the actual time elapsed to your estimated time. After jotting down your estimated time and effort, use a stopwatch to record your actual time and effort. The estimated and actual information may be close or vastly different. Experiment with how you can use the data you collect to make the changes needed to create a schedule that works for you.

ACTIVITY	ESTIMATED TIME AND EFFORT LEVEL	ACTUAL TIME AND EFFORT LEVEL	NOTES

Decision-Making

Decision-making is a complex and challenging process that requires that the brain use many of its executive functions at once to make a choice and move forward. Now, this is hard enough for people without ADHD, but when you pile on the traits and symptoms of ADHD—such as distractibility, hyperfocus, perfectionism, problem-solving difficulties, inflexibility, impulse control, and inhibition issues—decision-making can become an overwhelming and emotionally stressful event. It can lead to delays in making decisions, avoidance in making decisions altogether, or making a decision but feeling anxious and rethinking your choice and changing your mind, qualities that may appear to others as "flip-flopping." Of course, for an individual with ADHD, it is not done to be annoying; it is often due to the anxiety experienced when making a choice and then regretting it or ruminating about it. It can be a difficult cycle, leading to unproductive worrying, procrastination, and under-achievement, further feeding your negative thoughts and beliefs about yourself and fears of failure.

Here are what difficulties with decision-making may look like:

- Having many amazing ideas but having difficulty figuring out the best one to pursue based on the facts and information you have

- Starting crafts, hobbies, businesses, or other projects and abandoning them halfway because the idea of making the wrong decision and "failing" is too much to bear

- Distractibility or difficulty staying focused on narrowing down options—which turns an essential part of the decision-making process into a brainstorming process instead

- Leaving small and big decisions for your partner to determine because you cannot seem to commit to details (e.g., when to plan a date night, what activity you should do, where to make the reservation, etc.)

- Responding to invitations late, or not replying to invitations, texts, or emails at all

- Confirming plans only to cancel them at the last minute, or not showing up, because something else has come up and you cannot decide what is more pressing

- Losing opportunities due to taking too long to decide how to proceed

- Not starting a project at all because you feel stuck regarding where to go with it

- Paying higher fees or premiums for booking flights, hotels, or rental cars at the last minute, even though you have known about the event for a while

Difficulties with decision-making can be impairing for many reasons, and it is important to remind yourself that people do not dislike you as a person, but rather dislike what you do—or don't do—when it comes to getting stuff done. There is a big difference. If you get stuck, asking others how they make decisions, or working with someone—possibly your partner—to sit down and go through the mail, pay bills, and organize the home together—can be helpful. This allows you stay on task while having a social interaction—and using your talents to contribute to your personal and professional relationships in a meaningful way.

Coffee, Tea, or ???

Use this exercise to think about a decision you need to make, or practice using a decision you have made in the past—even a simple one like "Should I get coffee or tea?" The goal is to get into the habit of thinking of decision-making as a manageable skill, without having attachment to an outcome that is out of your control. Use this strategy anytime you notice you are procrastinating on tasks that require making decisions, big or small. Afterward, go do something fun to shift your attention from worrying about the outcome to getting something else done.

THE DECISION I NEED TO MAKE	
THE FACTS I KNOW	
PROS	
CONS	
POTENTIAL OUTCOMES	
THE DECISION I'M MAKING	

After looking at the decision in a systematic way, with all the facts I have now, my decision is:

....

....

....

Emotional Dysregulation vs. Irregularity

An important core feature of adult ADHD, although not yet officially included in the diagnostic criteria for ADHD, is emotional dysregulation, or difficulty with managing emotions appropriately in order to be able to continue getting things done without disruption. This issue affects people with ADHD daily and in every aspect of life, including work, school, relationships, and life aspirations.

People with ADHD experience emotions very deeply, and this intensity can be overwhelming for the brain, causing impulsive actions that lead to feelings of regret later. Common ways that emotional dysregulation may affect men with ADHD include:

- Consistently experiencing irritability and agitation

- Sudden and intense temper outbursts that seem out of context

- Easily losing interest in working toward a new goal at the first sign of difficulty, or frequently quitting jobs, projects, or social relationships

- Appearing apathetic or insensitive to the needs of others

- A low tolerance for stress or unanticipated changes

- Seeming withdrawn or disengaged at times

- Shifts in moods and feelings through the day, often unrelated to anything specific

- Sensitivity to others criticizing them or having a negative perception of them

- Rigid and inflexible thinking that makes it harder to adjust to change and come up with alternative strategies to address a persistent problem or challenge

- All-or-nothing thinking that prevents the ability to compromise

- Difficulty with perspective-taking that sometimes prevents cooperation with others

- Becoming defensive or angry If someone points out that something was done incorrectly

- Defaulting to automatic, negative self-talk or thoughts after getting an unfavorable response

Additionally, societal messages discourage men from expressing their emotions and suggest that being "emotional" is a weakness; therefore, many men grow up watching other men in their lives suppress their emotions, or not cope with them in a healthy way, and learn to do the same. Boys are often socialized to play with toy guns and action figures that perpetuate the value of physical strength over values such as kindness, compassion, and emotional intelligence. This is hard for men with ADHD, because they do experience a range of complex emotions, but they are not given opportunities to learn how to label and express their emotions to their advantage.

Emotional dysregulation can lead to divorce, increased conflicts in relationships with children, addiction, financial debt, frequent job losses or changes in jobs, and legal troubles.

Emotions drive creative, intuitive, bright, and artistic people—many of whom are men with ADHD. Learning to effectively manage strong emotions and using their power to be productive is essential for a healthy, balanced, and meaningful life. Practicing emotional regulation—such as through mindfulness or meditation—and increasing self-awareness of how your emotions are felt using a mind–body approach are both helpful techniques for addressing emotional dysregulation and achieving a calmer, happier, and more intentional life.

Being Present with Yourself

Mindfulness is a concept that encourages you to slow down and use your senses to increase your self-awareness and acceptance of yourself—without judgment, in the present moment, without needing to control or change anything. This can be hard at first and requires patience and effort, especially for individuals with ADHD. The key is to start slow, keep trying, and stick with it. There is no right or wrong way to do this. Approaching life with a mindful attitude can greatly support emotional growth and decrease challenges with emotional dysregulation, leading to a calmer and happier life.

The focus of this exercise is to be mindful: simply staying in the present moment by observing your thoughts and feelings—without judgment—and accepting things as they are.

1. Be present and mindful throughout your day. If you get distracted, notice the weather or the smells, sounds, textures, and sights in your immediate environment.

2. Notice when you feel overwhelmed, have a temper outburst, or have distressing feelings. Observe your thoughts, bodily sensations, feelings, and responses.

3. In the following table, record what happened during your day, including how you felt before and after you looked at your emotions in a mindful manner.

WHAT HAPPENED	
INTENSITY OF FEELINGS	
INTENSITY OF FEELINGS AFTER PRACTICING MINDFULNESS	
ADDITIONAL NOTES	

JAMIE'S STORY

Due to chronic tardiness and inconsistent work quality, Jamie was eventually let go from his job. He didn't know how or where to start looking for a new job, and eventually started feeling depressed and anxious regarding his future. In conversations with his family, he became defensive and felt tired. While unemployed, he tried to pick up new hobbies, only to spend money on supplies before losing interest in the hobby. His apartment was messy, with piles of clothes and paper everywhere. He began eating unhealthy food, with only sugar or carbs, and started skipping meals. Because he was unemployed, he was mostly in bed or on the couch and couldn't motivate himself to work out. He also admitted to drinking more during the day—the thing that prompted him to see his doctor. The doctor diagnosed Jamie with depression, prescribed antidepressants, and wrote him a referral for therapy. Jamie's attendance at therapy was inconsistent, and when he did attend sessions, he often felt misunderstood. He reported that the medication didn't work, and talking about his challenges wasn't helpful in making changes. Utterly frustrated, he really didn't understand why he couldn't "be normal and get it together."

One day, an acquaintance mentioned how she was recently diagnosed with adult ADHD and remarked that many of Jamie's challenges sounded similar to hers. Jamie followed up with the same clinician she had seen. He was assessed and diagnosed with ADHD, combined type, which led to the use of a different class of medications and behavioral therapy strategies, along with attending support groups. Jamie showed great improvement after starting the new medication and consistently attending individual and group therapy sessions. He learned to get organized, effectively manage his time, and be more self-aware. Within a few months of receiving his diagnosis and starting treatment, Jamie found a job he enjoyed, made a greater effort to stay in touch with friends and initiate plans, kept his commitments, and started dating again.

I can't always control what happens in life, but I can control how I react to it.

Key Takeaways

You now have a better idea of how the core symptoms of ADHD affect men in various aspects of life. ADHD is a complex condition that cannot be approached with a "one size fits all" mindset. Seeking out a clinician with expertise in adult ADHD diagnosis and treatment is an important step in working toward managing and minimizing the impacts of the challenging symptoms and traits of ADHD, while maximizing your strengths.

Here are a few things you can start doing now to help yourself:

- Keep a calendar that is always available to you and use it to record important information regarding recurring appointments and family member schedules—including notes about pickup and drop-off responsibilities, if you have kids—as well as scheduling chores and who is responsible for doing them on a given day. Prioritize important tasks with deadlines and do them first, when you have energy and uninterrupted time. It will take some time and effort, but making a commitment to sticking with your calendar, checking it, and updating it frequently is very important and will reap benefits.

- Cultivate a practice of living in a mindful way—one that helps you develop more self-awareness, compassion, and appreciation for what shows up for you or in you in the present moment, without judgment, so that you may live a calmer and more balanced life. Sometimes, just taking a deep breath in through the nose, with eyes closed, and counting the numbers 5-4-3-2-1 while breathing out through the nose, is all that's needed. Try doing this every hour, or as needed. It is an easy and simple way to start practicing mindfulness.

- Celebrate your success each day by writing down a positive interaction or event that made you feel good. Keep the notes in a "feel-good jar" or post them on a bulletin board to serve as motivation when you feel down or tired.

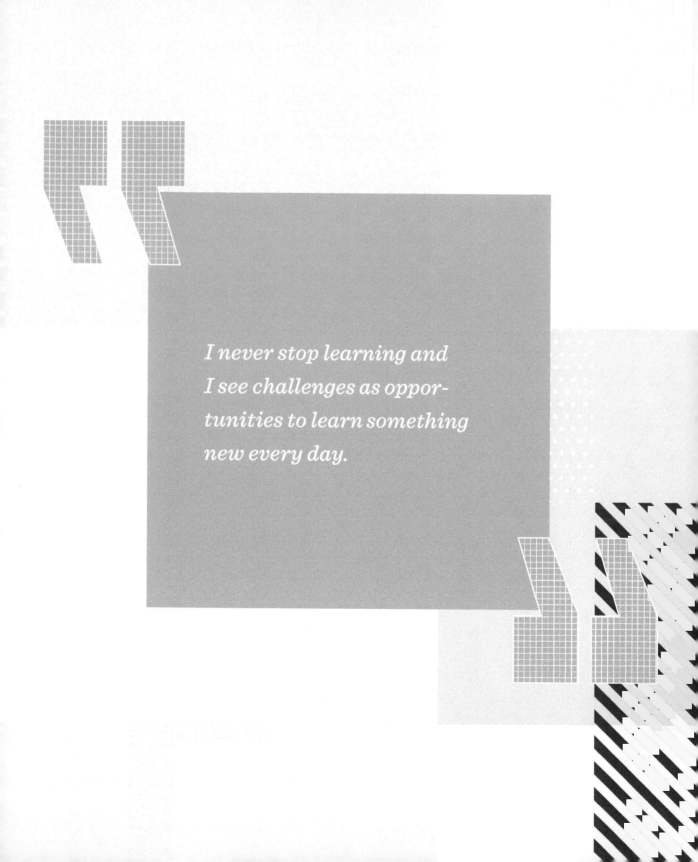

I never stop learning and I see challenges as opportunities to learn something new every day.

CHAPTER 2

Understanding ADHD

In the previous chapter, we looked at how the symptoms of ADHD impact men, and in what areas of their lives, while exploring how ADHD impacts you specifically. In this chapter, we will take a closer look at the core symptoms, associated features, and coexisting disorders of ADHD. We will take a deeper look at the executive functions and the role they play in ADHD, along with information on the many ways ADHD can manifest itself in your life. Some people experience severe impacts, whereas others are affected minimally or mostly in one area of life, but both can be very crushing for them and affect their daily functioning.

As much as possible, explore and absorb the information that you are about to read with an open mind, open heart, and compassion, knowing that your present does not have to be your future. In life, it is never too late to make positive changes that matter to you. If you feel happier, others you care about will feel better, too, all of which benefits society as well.

ALEX'S STORY

Alex is a social (yet shy with new people), creative, and artistic 20-year-old male. Growing up, Alex struggled academically. In class, he often left his seat to sharpen his pencil or talk to a peer. He struggled with math, often drew or doodled in his notebook during classes (when he attended them), and fidgeted frequently by crossing and uncrossing his legs, tapping his pencil, or pinching his arms or picking at scratches or scars. During adolescence, Alex avoided spending time at home and hung out with friends or smoked marijuana to deal with the stress and feelings of anxiety he frequently experienced. After leaving home to attend college in a large, urban city, Alex had difficulty adjusting to his new lifestyle, including doing his laundry, cooking, reminding himself to eat, and cleaning up messes in common areas, which led to conflicts with his roommates. Alex struggled to manage his emotions and finances effectively. He was frustrated with himself and often expressed feelings that indicated low self-esteem and self-defeating thoughts, which then became his perception of himself.

Eventually, Alex contacted the student health center at his college, which referred him to a clinician who happened to have expertise in assessing and diagnosing adult ADHD. After a thorough assessment process, a diagnosis was made of ADHD, combined type, with bipolar II mood disorder, associated depression, and anxiety secondary to ADHD. Alex's diagnoses were confirmed by a psychiatrist, and Alex was placed on stimulant medication and a mood stabilizer. Behavior therapy sessions addressed his underlying struggles—related to family dynamics and executive functioning skills deficits—to help him get organized, plan better, manage his emotions and finances better, and improve his work and social interactions. Health and lifestyle changes were also addressed to boost treatment outcomes in his favor. After three months of medication and consistent attendance, compliance, and participation in therapy sessions, Alex reported feeling good and more focused. He walked out of his last therapy session thankful for his journey, proud of himself for taking the steps needed to get his concerns addressed, and grateful to the clinicians who recognized the issues that were holding him back and applied an integrated and holistic approach to treating his ADHD.

What Is Adult ADHD?

Adult ADHD is a complex neurodevelopmental disorder comprised of many emotional and behavioral traits and symptoms that are a result of one's environment, genetics, different brain chemistry and wiring, and lack of certain neurotransmitters, such as dopamine (the feel-good/reward chemical), as well as societal expectations. There are three types of ADHD: inattentive, hyperactive-impulsive, and combined.

You cannot "grow out of" an ADHD diagnosis, but many men learn to compensate for their areas of difficulty by leveraging their strengths, which can include creativity, intelligence, innovativeness, and ambition.

Chronic challenges with the brain's inability to properly use executive functions are a major reason for the difficulties experienced, such as inattentiveness, impulsivity, lack of organization, improper task completion, procrastination, and poor time management. Repeated errors due to lack of attention to details or "zoning out" while directions are being provided can adversely affect personal and professional relationships and outcomes.

Learning to embrace your good, bad, and ugly selves without any judgment is an important mindset to adopt and skill set to cultivate because they can help propel you forward in life, toward reaching your goals, in an intentional and mindful way that is aligned with your values and beliefs.

Although all of this can seem overwhelming, there are medications, behavioral strategies, and social supports you can count on to help you get control over your ADHD symptoms and live the life that you want now.

The Many Faces of ADHD

ADHD can present itself in many different ways in different people. It is a disorder with a range of variability in the presentation of symptoms and in the experiences of people diagnosed with the disorder. How one man may present and cope with the core symptoms and associated features of ADHD, compared to another man with the same diagnosis depends on several complex factors, such as:

- Type of ADHD that is diagnosed

- Level of impairment experienced

- Social supports and resources available

- Cognitive development

- Family, health, and birth histories, including details regarding maternal health practices during pregnancy

- Environmental factors, such as exposure to toxins (e.g., lead), or family stress in the household

- Developmental history that includes trauma or PTSD (post-traumatic stress disorder)

- Societal messages received regarding traditional gender roles

- Cultural and religious beliefs regarding the use of medication and therapy to treat the core symptoms of ADHD

- Coexisting conditions, such as addiction or substance abuse, mood disorders, and/or anxiety

As you can see and most likely know by now, with an ADHD diagnosis, many complex and integrated factors have to be carefully considered in order to develop an effective treatment plan—which, for many individuals, can be life changing. Certain medications have been found to be highly effective in treating ADHD, along with consistent and targeted behavioral therapy techniques that implement environmental and behavioral modification strategies. Attending group therapy sessions has also helped many individuals, especially men, continue to make progress due to the social interaction the group provides. Individuals attending such sessions feel like they are not alone and have a supportive environment where they can share and process their emotions and feelings.

Key Takeaways

- ADHD is a neurodevelopmental disorder with three types: inattentive, hyperactive-impulsive, and combined.

- ADHD is often missed in childhood if inattentiveness is the way the symptoms appear, and it is sometimes misdiagnosed as depression or anxiety disorder in adults.

- There is no "one size fits all" approach, or a typical profile of what an adult man with ADHD presents as, so don't be discouraged if you don't see the changes you were hoping for right away after starting treatment. Be patient with yourself and trust the process. Keep notes to share with your health care provider or doctor regarding anything you notice after starting treatment, with or without medication.

- Symptoms and behavioral impacts can change over the course of one's lifespan, and sometimes even within a day or a week. This variability is part of the overall difficulty with self-regulation.

- Executive functions are essential skills coordinated by the brain, and include planning and organizing, time management, emotional regulation, working memory, and flexibility. These functions underlie key issues seen in individuals with ADHD and should also be addressed.

I will find the facts and follow the path of knowledge over ignorance.

Fact vs. Fiction: Debunking Common ADHD Myths

Although ADHD is well-known by name, there are many dated myths and misconceptions about it floating around, especially regarding adult ADHD and men. Increasing awareness and empowering adult men with ADHD to seek the emotional, psychological, social, and medical services they need to treat this brain-based disorder are essential in helping men replace shame and guilt with compassion and a willingness to see a different life, in which the strengths of ADHD can be included in their stories.

MYTH #1: ADHD is a made-up thing parents use to get their kids on meds that calm them down so they don't have to parent.

FACT: ADHD is a neurodevelopmental, or brain-based, disorder where executive function deficits lead to disorganization, impulsive behaviors, disinhibition, and inattentiveness, or high distractibility that impairs a person's ability to finish and start tasks, or remember what they were saying while walking. There are different levels of severity, and other disorders, such as depression and anxiety, and learning disabilities or differences, like dyslexia, can accompany ADHD.

MYTH #2: ADHD is a childhood disorder that badly behaved boys get and grow out of. So what's the big deal?

FACT: ADHD symptoms show up in childhood and can be diagnosed by a clinician with expertise and knowledge by the time a child is four years of age. Boys are diagnosed at higher rates because two of the ADHD subtypes, hyperactive-impulsive and combined type, present with more disruptive and observable behaviors while children are in school, and teachers are proactive in referring children for evaluation. Girls have ADHD, too, and many go undiagnosed in childhood until late adulthood due to symptoms presenting as predominantly inattentive type (a child stares out the window or doodles instead of taking notes); their ADHD goes unnoticed because they achieve average or passing grades or exhibit no disruptive behaviors. Society encourages girls to suppress disruptive behaviors, so they often learn to mask them at a young age. Their parents don't see the difficulties or normalize them because they have been living with unmanaged or undiagnosed ADHD their whole lives. A person cannot "grow out of it," but over the years, depending on how severe the symptoms are at the age of diagnosis, many individuals learn to compensate for the challenges and deficits. For instance, if dyslexia is present, a child may gravitate toward math and excel in that subject, or find a creative outlet that works for them. Unmanaged and undiagnosed ADHD can have severe implications for an individual, because it can lead to feeling unfulfilled, being underemployed, or underachieving and never really understanding why. They have been told to "just work harder" or "pay attention and you will get it" when in truth no amount of hard work can combat the challenges to learning that come with dyslexia, dyscalculia (difficulty with arithmetic), or dysgraphia (inability to write clearly) without special instruction and technology to help the student excel.

MYTH #3: You cannot be successful, have your own business, or get through college or medical school if you really have ADHD.

FACT: This is the most ignorant misconception because individuals with ADHD are usually highly intelligent, adaptive and resourceful, ambitious, creative, and sensitive. They have developed compensatory skills as part of the developmental process to keep up with their peers and the demands of their environment. Many thrive as entrepreneurs, are successful inventors, or are some of the greatest minds to have graced this earth, including Nobel Prize winners.

MYTH #4: Everybody has ADHD.

FACT: All individuals, at some point in their life, may display ADHD-like traits or symptoms. However, for their traits or symptoms to be considered a disorder, the ADHD has to cause dysfunction and enough impairment in an area of their life that, if left untreated, would be problematic for the individual and their family.

MYTH #5: ADHD is a rich-people disorder that wealthy parents made up to help get their kids extra time on tests so they could get into great colleges.

FACT: ADHD occurs in people across all genders, socioeconomic status, religions, and cultures. However, due to the complex nature of the disorder, stigmas associated with mental health care, and lack of awareness of or access to accurate information about ADHD, people of color, those with low incomes, and/or those who are likely to have lower levels of education often end up being left out of the diagnosis and treatment process. More often, boys of color receive the diagnosis in school when teachers notice their disruptive behavior. Immigrant parents face additional barriers such as language, lack of knowledge about special education laws, cultural traits that encourage conformity with authority figures, and lack of time due to long workdays, which isolate this population.

MYTH #6: ADHD is code for being lazy and unintelligent.

FACT: Brain scans have been done to compare the brains of people with ADHD and those without it. Studies have detected differences in the frontal lobe region of the brain and the parts of the brain associated with the reward system and emotional processing system. Additionally, lower levels of the neurotransmitter dopamine—the "rush" or "feel-good" brain chemical—in the frontal lobe confirms the need for individuals with ADHD to seek external stimulation through substances, high-risk activities like skydiving, or sex.

MYTH #7: ADHD was created by Big Pharma to keep selling drugs to people legally.

FACT: Stimulant medications that effectively treat the distractibility and impulsivity associated with ADHD are highly regulated and are not handed out like candy.

MYTH #8: You have to get neuropsychological tests done that cost thousands of dollars and receive a diagnosis from a psychologist to be considered as having a valid ADHD diagnosis.

FACT: Although specific psychological tests are useful in determining if there is a learning disability or cognitive delay present that needs to be addressed, no specific test is necessary to diagnose adult ADHD. The ADHD assessment process for adults usually follows a more holistic approach, where thorough information is collected by asking questions about an individual's medical, emotional, and social histories. Self-report rating scales, such as the Adult ADHD Self-Report Scale created by the American Psychiatric Association, are often used to gather information regarding functioning levels as per the 18 symptoms associated with the ADHD diagnosis in the DSM-5 (*Diagnostic and Statistical Manual of Mental Disorders*, Fifth Edition). Furthermore, detailed questioning and past report cards or work reviews are helpful in understanding the patterns of behaviors or areas of distress experienced over the years. Although different institutions can determine what their requirements are for accepting the ADHD diagnosis as being valid, it is not necessary that the diagnosis come from a psychologist or that a full neuropsychological battery of testing be done. What is important is for the clinician to have expertise in ADHD and its impact over the lifespan, an understanding of the tools to use and what to look for, and knowledge of the nuances of ADHD and the role emotional dysregulation plays in the disorder.

ADHD Self-Assessment

Complete the following self-report questionnaire based on your overall functioning over the past three months, rather than how you are feeling at this moment. After you are done, add up and record your total score. The higher your score, the more likely symptoms of ADHD are present.

If you are in treatment already, these results could shed light on progress or areas where you still need support. Pay particular attention to the areas where you checked "Always." Share this assessment with your doctor or clinician to discuss further and/or to assist in treatment management. Additionally, you could ask your partner or another person who knows you well to complete the questionnaire to get their perspective. You could then compare the scores to get a sense of the reliability of your self-reports, and also gain insight on what you may have overlooked or reported on negatively, but is not observed by others to have the negative impact you may have initially felt or thought. Either way, this assessment can give you clear insight regarding the areas you will want to work on.

ADULT ADHD SELF-REPORT QUESTIONNAIRE

HOW OFTEN DO YOU:	NEVER 0	SOMETIMES 1	ALWAYS 2
Have difficulty following through on the details of a task to wrap up a project after the main work is done?	☐	☐	☐
Make careless mistakes on forms, letters, tests, or time sheets, or while driving or doing chores around the house?	☐	☐	☐
Avoid getting started on projects that require multiple steps to complete?	☐	☐	☐
Forget important notes, dates, or obligations?	☐	☐	☐
Get easily distracted by noise or people around you?	☐	☐	☐
Lose focus on what you are doing when doing boring tasks?	☐	☐	☐

CONTINUED >

ADULT ADHD SELF-REPORT QUESTIONNAIRE

HOW OFTEN DO YOU:	NEVER 0	SOMETIMES 1	ALWAYS 2
Find yourself talking too much or interrupting others?	☐	☐	☐
Fidget or move around in your seat or find you can't sit still?	☐	☐	☐
Move around a room or go in and out when expected to stay seated?	☐	☐	☐
Pay late fees or struggle with managing finances?	☐	☐	☐
Have difficulty making or keeping friends?	☐	☐	☐
Have intense reactions that don't match the situation or are inappropriate to the context?	☐	☐	☐
Have conflicts with an intimate partner due to infidelity, not listening when they talk, being late to things, or forgetting chores?	☐	☐	☐
Have difficulty regulating and managing your emotions?	☐	☐	☐
Arrive late to events, meetings, work, or social gatherings?	☐	☐	☐
Start doing something and have trouble finishing it due to a distraction (e.g., stopping your work to read and reply to a personal email that pops up)?	☐	☐	☐
Have difficulty organizing and prioritizing your day?	☐	☐	☐
Buy things you don't need?	☐	☐	☐
Promise yourself or others you will get something done, but then can't seem to figure out how?	☐	☐	☐

Total score: ....

THE IMPORTANCE OF AN
OFFICIAL DIAGNOSIS

Getting an accurate and official diagnosis can be life-saving in the case of ADHD. A diagnosis can offer a solid treatment plan that includes: specific medications that address the ADHD neurochemical deficiencies first; individual behavior therapy and group therapy to help you understand the complex condition and its impact on you; and the development of positive coping strategies to address the psychological, social, and behavioral challenges you are experiencing. Furthermore, with a diagnosis you will be able to request reasonable workplace accommodations to help you do your job better, while feeling good about yourself and your career opportunities. Academically, you will be able to request special accommodations, including extended testing time, which can finally give you the chance to show your true capacities instead of the underachievement you had to settle for because the playing field wasn't even. Although the diagnosis should not be used as an excuse for poor behavior, it can help open a discussion regarding the difficulties in your relationships, giving you a chance to work on them and be happier. Embracing your diagnosis of ADHD and all that comes with it, while willing to be vulnerable and get the right help, can be a transformational experience.

The ADHD assessment questionnaire you just completed was created to be used as a tool to help you examine and understand how ADHD impacts you and to what extent. It is a great starting point and gives you something you can take to your next doctor's appointment or therapy session to facilitate further discussions regarding your findings.

Please keep in mind that the questionnaire is not intended as a replacement for an official diagnosis and treatment from a licensed health care provider qualified to diagnose and treat ADHD. It should be regarded only as a helpful tool.

Key Takeaways

Congratulations for sticking with and completing chapter 2! You now have a better understanding of adult ADHD in men and, through the questionnaire, hopefully a better understanding of how the specific symptoms of ADHD impact you.

- ADHD is a brain-based disorder that presents with deficits in executive functions, with its core symptoms being distractibility, hyperactivity, impulsivity, and emotional dysregulation. Review the questionnaire again and see what comes up for you as you go over the findings. Share your findings and thoughts with your doctor to see what you can do to live a more fulfilling life based on your definition of success.

- Several myths keep men from accessing a proper diagnosis and treatment for a very treatable chronic condition. Media, misinformation, pop culture, and medication commercials have created an image of ADHD that is way too simplistic for a complex disorder that has significant impacts on people's lives. You don't have to share your diagnosis or justify it to anyone else, so don't let that stop you from getting the care you deserve and need to live your best life. And the next time you hear someone make a joke about the validity of ADHD or state a myth, feel free to debunk it—calmly, of course!

- Receiving an official diagnosis is important and gives you access to helpful resources in the workplace and academic settings to help you be more effective and efficient and to thrive. You can schedule an appointment with your human resources representative to discuss the Americans with Disabilities Act and what the next steps are regarding accommodations. For instance, perhaps a later start time, allowing you to get a little more sleep in the morning, is just what you need. In a school setting, go to the counseling office to inquire further about your options. Find out if low-cost testing to assess ADHD is available to you as a student through your counseling center.

I will use my strengths to overcome my difficulties.

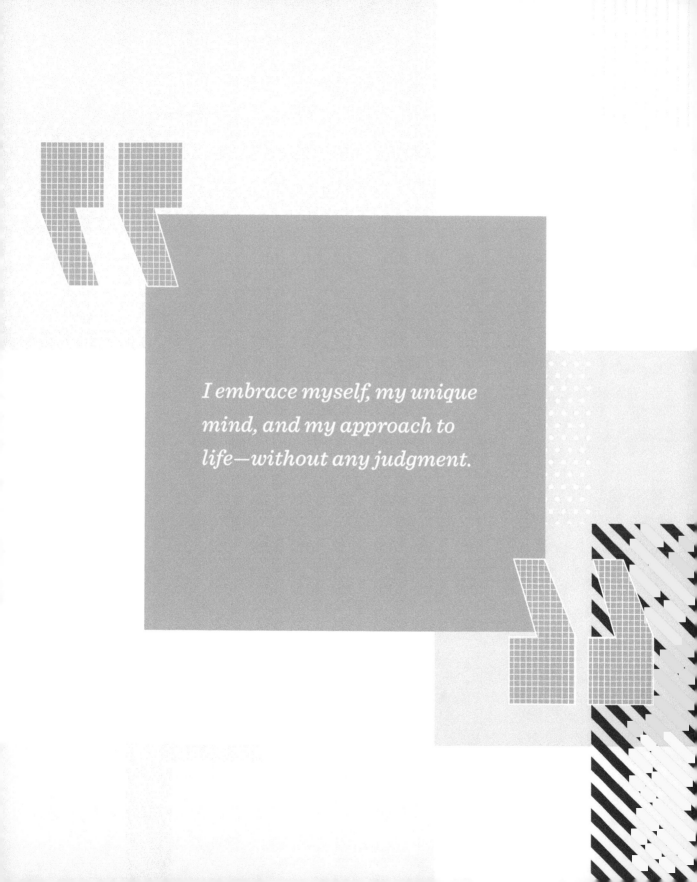

I embrace myself, my unique mind, and my approach to life—without any judgment.

CHAPTER 3

Embracing Your Neurodivergence

The focus of this chapter is on reflecting on your strengths and challenges, and accepting and embracing your unique mind. Of course, there will be challenging days when the disorder may seem overwhelming and it is hard for you to see the positives embedded in your struggles. It is important to understand that acceptance does not mean invalidating your experiences. Acceptance in this context is about being able to see yourself having the thoughts you have and letting them be, as opposed to *being* the thoughts. This may seem difficult, but with practice it is possible to view struggles through this lens so that you can grow and neutralize the strong emotions that may prevent you from accomplishing your goals.

The essential goal of this chapter's information and exercises is to help you use your brain's wiring to find opportunities in your professional and personal realms, along with ways to adjust the environment to work for you, versus trying to fit into a structure that may not be well suited to where you are right now. Things are changing and there is more awareness about the needs of adults with ADHD as a neurodivergent population. However, there are also things you can do to embrace your unconventional or nontraditional ways of doing things and empower yourself to reach your goals, instead of trying to fit into an existing blueprint. The reality is that the way most people work—at home and in an office—may not work best for you, and you don't have to do it that way. Learning to neutralize the challenges your symptoms present while harnessing the power of your unique strengths will allow you to reach your desired outcomes.

By using your creativity and resourcefulness, you can find a way to do what you love and do it on your (or mostly your) own terms to create a healthy balance. We will explore that further in this chapter.

At work or in personal settings, Edi noticed that his ideas were met with skepticism and criticism most of the time. Edi was always taught to speak softly and not draw too much attention to himself, so he wondered if people didn't hear him. Edi also often avoided eye contact. Over time, like when planning a trip, his friends ended up uninviting him because of his "overplanning." Edi would feel extremely hurt by the rejections. In team meetings at work, Edi often strayed from the agenda or didn't ask questions, and then tasks were left undone. He would also pitch new ideas and projects during meetings focused on the logistics of a project already in progress. Repeated gentle nudges, or even statements such as "That is a great idea for another time, but let's get back to this issue at hand" went over Edi's head and he would stay focused on his idea. Confusion, frustration, and resentment were building up. Edi had days when he would stay home from work without calling in. Human resources reached out to reprimand him, but after the representative took time to understand the issues, she connected Edi with the company's employee assistance program. Edi followed up on this, which led to pivotal leaps in his journey with ADHD.

Working with, Not against, Your Mind

One of the reasons you may feel out of place or unsuccessful sometimes is the expectation to fit in. That expectation runs counter to the way most individuals with ADHD like to do things. In fact, the same traits that disrupt the organized, time-focused, and traditional society we live in are the same ones that also make you excel and stand out. Clarifying your understanding of your needs, strengths, and weaknesses, along with your passion and purpose, is important. By knowing yourself, you will realize when you have found what you are looking for, while maintaining realistic expectations and managing your emotions in an adaptive way.

Self-awareness can drive success because you can direct your energy toward what you are good at and make decisions based on facts and intuition to get a positive result. The ADHD mind thrives on praise and validation, so seek out environments where they are provided and allow you to feel pride in yourself. Your mind is self-critical, so balancing it out with positive self-talk and cultivating self-compassion is healthy and necessary.

Quick thinking and seeing things from a unique perspective, especially when under pressure, are skills many professions and companies actively seek out. If your academic record wasn't (or isn't) stellar—because of the distractibility or learning differences that accompany ADHD—know that it's not that you are unintelligent or incompetent, but rather that you have, and have had, more hurdles to jump through than other people before you even get to the starting line. Keep that in mind when your thoughts lead you down a negative spiral; instead, imagine going up the spiral and beginning at the same starting line as others. You may notice other people have challenges as well—we all do. Theirs may be different from yours, but the way someone else experiences a challenge might be similar to how you feel when you are late for an event or can't meet a deadline.

Many schools and large corporations are considering new hiring and admissions practices that are more inclusive and don't exclude neurodivergent people based on scores and grades, or how they perform during an interview. These changes come with the realization that there are amazing benefits to having neurodivergent individuals on a team, due to their action-oriented task execution during a crisis, hyperfocus on details that otherwise might be overlooked, and perfectionism tendencies that result in high-quality work. Such individuals make good employees who waste less time socializing once they are into the work and feel supported and appreciated.

With ADHD, it's about not being able to do what you already know how to do. Anxiety, stress, and depression can impact your capacity to cope with uncomfortable emotions or bad days by making you feel stuck in the distress and stalling you from finishing what you were working on. Every time you experience intense emotions, acknowledge them and observe what your thoughts are, but try to stay detached and not react. Just accept what is. Connect the mind and body to feel it, without internal dialogue that may jump to the worst-case scenario—which may or may not happen. Learning to recognize how ADHD influences you is a great starting point, letting you develop a game plan to address the challenges you encounter and further cultivate your strengths. Try to choose a career that provides flexibility, variety, and excitement. Choose friends and other relationships that stimulate your mind, are reciprocal, and make you smile because you know you have support.

As mentioned before, there is no "one size fits all" solution because there is no single profile that fits every person with ADHD. One thing that is clear is that neurodivergence is a trait, like being left-handed or right-handed. There is nothing wrong with you—your talents are great—and learning to harness the ADHD brain can lead to many opportunities. There is effective treatment out there, and professionals who specialize in adult ADHD will be able to understand your strengths and difficulties, and help you identify how to best use all that you bring to this world while feeling like you are part of it, and not an outsider.

I will give myself the same kindness and compassion that I give my loved ones.

Key Takeaways

- Embrace and accept yourself for who you are and what you bring with you, in the moment, without any judgment. Slow down your mind so you can hit the brakes in time, before an impulsive decision derails your relationships, career, or other endeavors. Reinforce positive experiences over negative ones, so you can see life from a more balanced perspective, instead of seeing it as all bad or all good. Allow others to know your struggles so they can help you, just as you can help them with theirs.

- In your relationships, personal or professional, strive to be around people who help you feel better yet hold you accountable for your actions. Be around people who will help you or offer support, as opposed to criticizing you for difficulties you know you have and are working on—you are hard enough on yourself already. Be open and willing to communicate your needs with people and be ready to listen with a curious and quiet mind when others are talking to you. Ask questions and be accepting of diverse thoughts and beliefs when it comes to a topic you are passionate about.

- Embrace, love, and accept all of yourself—including all the positives and negatives that come with ADHD and its related concerns. Direct your mind to be in the present moment and guide your energy and attention with the question, "What am I doing right now and why?"

What works for everyone else may not always work for me, and that's okay.

JESSI'S STORY

Through consultation with a psychiatrist who specialized in ADHD, Jessi was able to find a good medication regimen, therapy, and a support group for men with adult ADHD. Jessi felt better after meeting others with similar challenges and learning that ADHD was more common than he thought. It was especially interesting for Jessi to learn about the many men who didn't get diagnosed with ADHD until much later in life, because they weren't running around the classroom or jumping up and down when sitting down was expected. In therapy, he explored his feelings regarding a diagnosis that validated his struggles and allowed him to feel compassion for the years of feeling like a social misfit because of tardiness, moods that impacted relationships and career goals, and being called lazy and unintelligent—when his intelligence wasn't the issue. Over time, he learned to channel his ability to initiate projects and see them through with the help of a therapist, a mentor at work, and friends who helped Jessi stay accountable and didn't try to distract him. Self-medicating, with alcohol or pills not prescribed for him, stopped because he was able to learn how to cope with intense emotions and keep going despite the feelings. The ADHD medication worked well for him—though it took a few trials to find the right dose—and he felt like he was on an even playing field with his peers for the first time in his life.

Learning to Embrace Your Quirks

Rather than dimming your light to fit in, take a second to consider what the possibilities could be if you let yourself be you. That means accepting and embracing the challenging parts of yourself along with the positive parts. Leverage your positive traits, such as creativity, intuition, charismatic personality, passion for creating change, and leadership—traits that most trailblazers have. Instead of pushing away your unique perspectives and strong personality traits, use them to your advantage and make them work for you. Challenge yourself to see yourself in different ways; impulsivity can be seen as taking action decisively, whereas reactivity can mean being passionate about something and really investing yourself in the project you are working on.

If college or completing a higher degree was not something you were interested in, that is not the end of the world. You can use your talents and go for a professional certification that will give you the skills you need to advance at your job. Alternatively, if going to college was a dream but you were unable to attend due to low academic performance in high school because of ADHD-related issues, consider applying now or attending classes through a hybrid or online program that can give you the flexibility and support you need as a working professional and adult.

Determine what values or characteristics move you and encourage yourself to show up as your whole self—professionally and personally—without guilt or embarrassment. There are occupations that have variable schedules, start later, or have night hours—which are perfect for embracing the night owl in you. Some occupations provide the opportunity to do different things from one day to the next. People with an ADHD mind often thrive in crisis situations and think more clearly where others panic. There are high-adrenaline occupations that might serve you well and allow you to develop a sense of belonging and connection to others by helping them and being grateful for your life at the same time. Or you can be your own boss and start that side hustle or business you have been meaning to get into—but talk with someone knowledgeable about the field first, of course. Allow yourself to explore what works for you and how you can be your best self. As with anything you do, this can help make the highs feel better and the lows feel less intense. Make friends with yourself and urge yourself to respond to your misses with the same compassion you would show to your partner or a friend, while celebrating your hits with the same enthusiasm you would celebrate theirs.

You Don't Have to Do Things Like Everyone Else

As mentioned earlier, the way most people work is not what works for you, but that is completely fine. Everyone has different ways of doing things. Successful people recognize their strengths and use them to build up areas of weaknesses and delegate the work they are not great at doing. The time saved can then be invested in things that matter to them, such as friends, family, and hobbies. You might think about doing something similar. Consider sending your laundry or dry cleaning to a business that offers pickup and drop-off; automate your bill paying to avoid late fees; go paperless to avoid accumulating piles of paper. You can even have groceries delivered to you on a regular basis if going to the store makes you feel overwhelmed. Reduce repetitive and mundane tasks that you don't enjoy—or send them out.

Anytime you hear yourself say, "I should be able to . . . " remind yourself that everyone needs help with something, and certain businesses and services exist expressly to meet those needs; one of the luxuries of living in today's world is that there are services that fit all budgets and needs. Don't get stuck trying to paint your entire house if that is not your skill set. Especially consider outside help if you lose track of time or a particular task leads to frustration, causing your mood to go from positive to negative, and possibly leading to you missing a prior commitment that should have been a priority. Automate, delegate, and replicate to save yourself time and physical and emotional energy. Then invest that time and energy in doing things you enjoy, like seeing friends and family you care about.

When you start a new project, draft an outline that works for you and follow it. But make sure your goals and objectives are realistic and doable. Setting unrealistic goals is the fastest way to go down a negative spiral, completely sabotaging your efforts. When in doubt, have a helpful friend or colleague review your plan to make sure it sounds feasible or suggest changes if it is not. Create for yourself the mental and physical conditions in which you work best.

Ultimately, the meaning of success is different for everyone, and your definition may change many times during your life. Money isn't the only measure. Success is also about the quality of your life, the relationships you have, and feelings of joy and contentment. There are many paths that lead to a successful life, and it is up to you to decide what matters most. Although it is easier said than done, it *is* possible to make small changes in how you live your life. When you do, longer-term changes will follow.

Mindful Self-Talk

Thoughts are products of the mind, not facts or direct indicators of what is true. Observe your thoughts and self-talk today. Notice the thoughts your mind has about you, your relationships, your career, and anything else that comes up. Notice the impact these thoughts have on your sense of self. Practice noticing these thoughts and study them with curiosity, without being completely absorbed in them.

When you make a mistake today, no matter how big or small, treat yourself like you are someone you love dearly. How would you respond if your loved one did something similar? Use this as a prompt to write yourself a letter through friendly eyes. How does it feel to be friendlier toward yourself? Encourage yourself to be more self-compassionate and practice this the next time you make a mistake, professionally or personally.

Key Takeaways

Now that you have a better understanding of the things you can do to embrace your neurodivergence, start applying the idea of using mindfulness-based activities to accept yourself and the moment, as is. Also remember to automate, delegate, and replicate to make life easier for yourself and find ways to do more of what you love and less of what you don't like. Use the following action steps to help you move forward.

- Take note of your most important values. For example, perhaps you value serving others or sharing love with family. Now take a look at your schedule for the upcoming week. Are you spending time on things you find meaningful and care about, or are urgent or trivial things crowding out what's important? After you review your schedule, find one way today to align your values with your calendar. Do the same tomorrow.

- Keep a list of things you do that you wish you didn't have to do and look for ways you can automate, delegate, or replicate them easily. For example, ask friends or neighbors for referrals if you are looking for a specific service, or do a quick search online and call.

- Practice ways to manage your emotions and presence in the moment by using your breath to guide you. Whether you are sitting at your desk, sitting on the floor, or lying down, take a deep breath through your nose and imagine a bright light clearing your body of any aches, tension, or stress. Then release the breath through your nose down toward your feet. Do this for one to two minutes or for as many breaths as you are comfortable with. Every time you take a breath, perform a stretch along with it. Think of something you are grateful for—your family, partner, pet, friends, parents, job, school, or just the breath—as you do this.

- Make friends with time instead of seeing it as an enemy you are constantly fighting with. Give yourself some time on the weekend when you don't have to watch the clock, and engage in an activity you enjoy (listening to podcasts, hiking, something creative and artistic, writing, etc.). Let yourself go with the flow, and feel joy and contentment as you learn to embrace time as an ally.

There's more than one right way to do something.

CHAPTER 4

Quick and Easy Strategies You Can Start Using Now

As discussed in chapter 1, executive functions are abilities used to plan and organize, problem-solve, control impulses to keep you on task, and manage your emotional responses to situations. These important skills are controlled by the brain. If you feel overwhelmed (or curious, happy, sad, frustrated), know that there are many things you can explore to address executive dysfunction, including medication, behavioral therapy, and environmental modifications. It may be helpful for you to know that medication is an important part of the treatment for ADHD and addresses executive dysfunction for the amount of time the medication dosage is active in your system. You can think of taking medication for executive dysfunction as similar to having to wear contact lenses to correct poor eyesight.

Beyond medication, you will need other supports in place to deal with executive dysfunction, and that is what this chapter is all about—providing practical, easy-to-implement strategies that you can get started with right away. Remember, executive functions have nothing to do with willpower or laziness. Executive dysfunction is a brain-based chemical and wiring issue that is out of your control. Even individuals who do not have attention or hyperactivity challenges get tired and lose their focus and willpower as the day goes on and more energy is spent on low-stimulation tasks, as well as addressing matters such as hunger, sleep, and so on.

The key is to integrate strategies to address the executive function deficiencies into your daily life so they become habits. Habits are easier for your brain to do automatically, while requiring less energy and effort from you.

Additional tips and strategies that you can add to your ADHD toolkit are provided at the end of this chapter.

SAM'S STORY

Sam was excited to host a dinner for friends and was going to cook for everyone. The decision to host the dinner was spontaneous, leaving little time for planning the details and grocery shopping. Feeling excited and happy, Sam went to start the prep in the kitchen only to realize he forgot the chicken for the chicken casserole. Sam immediately tossed a plate and reached for a prescription pill for anxiety he got from a friend and the bottle of wine meant to be enjoyed with dinner. Negative thoughts started swirling in his head as he remembered his past "failures," including a replay of his visit to the grocery store where he recalled seeing the chicken but got distracted, lost track of time, and ultimately forgot to pick it up. Unable to move forward, Sam canceled plans 30 minutes before the event. His friends were disappointed and pointed out his pattern of doing this, and he never heard from a few of those friends again. It took a while, but Sam was able to reconnect with a few friends who were willing to listen to him and were understanding and supportive. They helped him get organized and find a therapist to work with, and scheduled plans for a weekly coffee get-together or a quick dinner out at a restaurant. They also helped Sam stay accountable by picking him up for their outings if Sam was thinking of canceling last minute.

Your Strategy Toolkit

This section contains useful, practical, and easy-to-implement strategies you can start using right away. These coping strategies, tips, and techniques address various challenges that come with ADHD and make it difficult for you to show the world what you know. Rather than requiring you to adopt a brand-new system or change your entire way of life, these strategies are intended to blend into your current lifestyle. That is important because individuals with ADHD thrive when they get feedback from their actions right away, as opposed to two months later. Repetition, consistency, and focusing on progress can boost your success. You are encouraged to try out all the strategies and keep doing them as often as you can, at work, at home, in social settings, or anywhere that makes sense for you. Doing so can lead to long-term success, increased confidence, and mastery of all you know you can do—starting now, at whatever point you are at in your life.

These strategies are designed to fit into your day by helping you make small changes that provide short-term, immediate benefits, ones that can develop into long-term habits that evolve with you, including how to manage procrastination, your time, your emotions, and schedules by using your strengths. This part of the book is definitely hands-on—you learn the strategies and then implement them at your own pace to get your rhythm going. As you probably know, the biggest challenge is often getting started. But once you do, the results you see will keep you going.

For Procrastination

- **GET MOVING:** If you are avoiding doing something due to a perceived difficulty and a low energy level, go for a short run, bike ride, swim, or do anything that gets your heart rate up. These activities release "happy" brain chemicals, like endorphins, serotonin, and dopamine, that shift mood states into balance. Also, engaging in exercise or physical movement before beginning a task that requires mental concentration makes it more likely you will be able to resist distractions.

- **DO IT NOW:** Whenever you have something to do, use the five-second rule: Do a countdown from five to one and then get started. It is likely that if you wait longer than that, you won't get around to doing it. Think of something you need to do that you have been avoiding, such as going through a pile of mail. Go to that space, tell yourself, "I need to sort mail now," count backward from five, and then do it!

- **STEP IT UP:** If starting something is hard because you feel overwhelmed by the energy and effort it will require, start with the first step today, like placing the stack of mail you need to go through on your desk. Tomorrow, go through the mail and immediately toss out the junk mail. The next day, go through three important pieces of mail and do what is required, like writing a check, putting it in the outgoing mail pile, and so on. By breaking up tasks this way, over time it will become easier to tackle them and get things done!

Purpose Behind Procrastination

Complete this exercise to explore your reasons for procrastinating. Identifying which tasks you avoid or delay starting can lead to insight and self-awareness about the executive functions you need to address. For example, if you realize you procrastinate across the board when it comes to paperwork, chances are it is because of issues with planning and organization. Or, if you end up with clutter you can't seem to let go of, it could be a fear of forgetfulness that makes you hold on to things "just in case."

The tasks I avoid doing or delay starting are (fill in each area):

WORK	
FAMILY LIFE	
SOCIAL LIFE	
PERSONAL GOALS	
OTHER	

The themes or similarities I see among these areas are related to (check off each relevant category):

☐ Finances ☐ Attention and concentration

☐ Social interactions ☐ Perfectionism

☐ Strong emotions ☐ Mundane routines

☐ Organizing and planning ☐ Other: _____

☐ Time management

The skills I need to learn or get better at based on these findings include:

_____

_____

_____

_____

_____

_____

_____

_____

_____

_____

For Time Management

- **WRITE IT DOWN IN ONE PLACE:** Keep a large wall calendar where you write down everything you know you and/or your family members do each day, including kids' classes, social events, and trips; also note work hours and school hours. Make it a habit to check the calendar every evening so you can prepare for the next day and update things as they change. You can also use an online calendar or a portable calendar you can take with you wherever you go, where you can record or write down meetings and events, along with the important tasks you need to get done that day.

- **"DO IT NOW" LIST:** Every morning, review your schedule and pick out three things you absolutely need to get done that day. Focus on completing those three things before doing anything else, including looking through emails or messages.

- **CLOCKS, VISUALS, AND TIMERS:** Use visual cues, like a whiteboard or sticky notes placed in your view, to remind you of the important tasks you need to do that day, or even just the task you are currently working on, so you can stay focused. You can place these visual aids in various places around your space to remind you of tasks you frequently forget to do, like locking the door. Keep digital clocks visible to keep you in the habit of checking the time, and set alarms to remind you when you need to stop doing one thing and transition to another.

Command Your Day

This activity will help you get started in setting up your "command center" and schedule.

1. Decide whether you want to primarily use an electronic calendar, a physical planner you will keep with you at all times, or a wall calendar. Pick the one you think will work best for you.

2. Choose the area that will be your "command center"; this is where you will hang your wall calendar. It's useful to choose a space that you pass by often. Don't spend too much time on this; just take a few minutes to consider it. You can change the area later if it is not working for you, but give it a consistent try for at least three months. If you have decided to use an electronic calendar or a physical planner, be sure to copy the information entered on them onto your wall calendar in your command center. Writing down the information again will (1) help reinforce the dates and events in your mind and (2) provide a visual when you are making plans and preparing for the following day. For most individuals with ADHD, having a command center helps them stay organized, be on time, and be prepared.

3. Make a list of the things you will need (e.g., a planner if you are keeping your schedule with you, a large whiteboard you can put on the wall, markers, notebooks, pens, etc.).

4. Fill in your schedule for the next seven days, starting with the day you are preparing it. Even if you are waiting for your supplies, get your schedule down on paper or in a calendar app for now and then transfer it later, if necessary. Use the following space to get started, if you wish. Check your schedule regularly throughout the week and take notes as you try to figure out what works best for you. Continue to personalize your schedule—and own it!

CONTINUED >

DAY 1

DAY: .... TIME: ....

ACTIVITY/TASK: ....

NOTES: ....

....

DAY 2

DAY: .... TIME: ....

ACTIVITY/TASK: ....

NOTES: ....

....

DAY 3

DAY: .... TIME: ....

ACTIVITY/TASK: ....

NOTES: ....

....

DAY 4

DAY: .... TIME: ....

ACTIVITY/TASK: ....

NOTES: ....

....

DAY 5

DAY: .... TIME: ....

ACTIVITY/TASK: ....

NOTES: ....

....

DAY 6

DAY: .... TIME: ....

ACTIVITY/TASK: ....

NOTES: ....

....

DAY 7

DAY: .... TIME: ....

ACTIVITY/TASK: ....

NOTES: ....

....

For Disorganization

- **CLEAR THE CLUTTER:** Pick a small space or room that you need to clean up and organize. Set a timer for 15 minutes and pick a small thing to start with. When the timer goes off, take a 5-minute break, then continue with another part of the room or with the task you started on. Keep in mind that doing something for 2 minutes is better than doing nothing, so start with a time that is realistic for you and build up from there. Turn this into a habit by picking one space or room that needs to get organized every day.

- **LABELS AND NOTES:** To keep things organized, find a place for everything and make sure an item goes back to that place when you are done with it. Create some labels for bins, kitchen containers, and drawers. Again, start with one thing that won't take too much time but that gets you engaged doing it—this makes it more likely you will continue.

- **ONE IN, TWO OUT:** Limit what you purchase, and buy things that serve more than one purpose for you. For example, buy a chair or coffee table that has storage space where you can tuck away your TV remote, books, magazines, or loose clutter. Or buy a magnetic whiteboard you can write messages on, and where you can also use magnets to post to-do lists or important notices or bills so they stay in sight. Before you buy something, think about where you want to put it and what you can toss out or donate before buying it. For every one item you purchase, let two similar things go.

Divide and Declutter

Clutter can build up and create a feeling of chaos. For ADHD brains, clutter can cause issues with inattention, distractibility, and hyperactive/impulsive actions. The ADHD mind will focus on what is in front of it, so clutter can be very distracting. Dealing with clutter does not mean you have to throw everything away; however, you will have to part with a few things.

Using the following grid, go through your living space and take inventory of each room's orderliness, layout, and level of clutter. Check to see if there are items that need to be reorganized; if there are, make a list of these items and consider whether you can donate them or toss them instead. Once you are done, review your notes and write down the date and time you will address each area.

ROOM	WHAT I NEED TO DO IN THIS SPACE	HOW I WILL DO THIS	WHEN I WILL DO THIS
BEDROOM			
KITCHEN			
LIVING/FAMILY ROOM			
BATHROOM			
OTHER			

For Indecision

- **JUST CHOOSE SOMETHING:** Not everything deserves to be thought about for a long time, and it really simplifies your life if you just pick something, stick with it, and then let it be. For everyday choices, like a lunch order, pick something within two minutes or flip a coin to help you choose and then stick with your choice. Done! And keep in mind, if you end up not liking what you ordered today, you don't have to have it tomorrow. Save your energy for the things that matter most to you.

- **KNOW YOUR MEANING:** For adults with ADHD, passion for what they are doing is incredibly important. When you're trying to make a decision that isn't so simple, jot down a few thoughts about why you're making this decision or what it means to you. Think about what may be getting in the way of making the decision, or making it difficult to stick with once you've made it. If you can't figure out all the details, that's okay; but if you have a sense of the direction you want to go in, keep trying to stick with it before you decide it doesn't work. If it needs changing, shake things up and figure out what might help make it work better.

- **NOW AND LATER:** Write down the short- and long-term pros and cons of a choice. Sometimes the long-term pros can be worth pursuing. It may mean giving up some short-term gratification, but you can always give yourself a reward from time to time as you work to reach your longer-term goal.

Working Backward

When it comes to ADHD, making decisions (big or small) can turn into a distracting and overwhelming process. Sometimes working backward helps. Start by understanding what you want the outcome to look and feel like, then "plug in" your options to see if they provide the outcome you want by asking yourself some questions to get clarity. Use the following prompts to develop a framework that you can apply when you feel stuck in your decision-making process.

What decision am I making?	
When do I need to make this decision by?	
Is this a small or big decision?	
What relevant facts do I know?	
Will this decision have a short-term or long-term impact on me?	
What do I want the outcome to be? **(START HERE AND WORK BACKWARD)**	

For Impulsivity

- **YOUR IMPULSIVITY IS NOT ABOUT WILLPOWER:** Your mind is faster than your ability to put the brakes on something you are doing, even if it's something you know will be a bad choice, or you recognize that after the fact. When this happens, realize and accept that what you did wasn't the best decision, but don't brood on it. That will only make you increase your negative thoughts about yourself or the situation. Instead, recognize what happened, accept account-ability, think about what can you do differently next time, and move on. It can be helpful to make a list of these steps and post it somewhere you can always see it, or always keep it on you, so you'll know what to do when you start to think about doing something that is not in your best interest.

- **MANAGING YOUR STRESS:** Using your emotions and logic together is important. Plan your day with care, manage stressors or try to anticipate them, and think of ways you can diffuse a stressful situation. For example, try to maintain a regular routine, put things in the same place each time so you can find them easily, follow a mindfulness or yoga practice, or spend more time in nature or with a pet. Realize that no matter what, some things will always be out of your control—and that's okay.

- **MEDICATION:** Medication is a powerful tool to help manage impulsivity by addressing the lower levels of some brain chemicals found to be important in managing impulsivity and reactivity. However, medication only works while the dose is in your system, so try to do your important tasks when you take your medication, can stay seated, and can concentrate.

Tame Your Triggers

Impulsive behaviors can get you into a lot of trouble with your boss, friends, family members, and/or the law, making effectively managing impulsivity an important skill to master. In most cases, it's important to work on the underlying causes—the triggers—that motivate verbal, emotional, or behavioral impulsivity. A *trigger* is a stimulus—such as a person, place, situation, or thing—that contributes to an unwanted emotional or behavioral response.

Use this exercise to put the previously discussed strategies into practice.

- Reflect on the problem your triggers are contributing to. What's the worst-case scenario if you are exposed to your triggers? With impulsivity, it can be hard to manage your reactions in the moment sometimes, so it's crucial to have a plan in place to prevent yourself from acting on your impulsivity.

- Just about *anything* can be a trigger. To begin exploring your own triggers, think about each of the following categories listed. Is there a specific emotion that acts as a trigger for you? How about a person or place in your environment? Write your responses in the space provided.

EMOTIONAL STATE	
PHYSICAL STATE	
ON/OFF MEDICATION	
ENVIRONMENT	

CONTINUED >

THOUGHTS	
ACTIVITIES/ SITUATIONS	

Now think of three things you can do to stop yourself from acting impulsively (e.g., finding a distraction, deep breathing, reading sticky notes with phrases that remind you to stay on task). Record them here:

1)

2)

3)

For Anger or Emotional Volatility

- **REFER TO YOUR SCALE:** Before you respond or take action when presented with an issue, imagine the issue on a scale from 1 to 5, where 1 is not a big deal and 5 is a very big deal. Take a deep breath, count to five, and then ask yourself where on that scale the issue falls. If you determine it's a level 2 issue, then responding with a level 5 answer doesn't match the context. It will take practice, but once you start to incorporate this strategy into your process of responding to issues and daily activities, it will become easier to use and you will see improvements in how you react.

- **CREATE A GAME PLAN:** Before going into a situation that you have identified as being stressful or overwhelming for you, write down what the worst-case outcomes look like. Next, plan for them by practicing what you can say or do to redirect a conversation, exit an interaction gracefully, or know when you need to leave (especially if you are experiencing physical symptoms that usually lead to a temper outburst or regrettable action). The key is learning to understand where you struggle in specific situations or why they feel overwhelming so you can put some strategies in place and practice them before exposing yourself to those situations.

- **BE FLEXIBLE:** When you are engaged in a disagreement or argument, stop and try to see the issue from the other perspective. Remind yourself that not everyone thinks like you and listen to the other person's point of view with curiosity. Ask questions to find out if you can learn something new, and respond accordingly instead of reacting immediately. If you have a hard time, practice your exit lines, like "Let's just agree to disagree," and change the topic. Also, if possible, avoid topics that are nonnegotiable for you—that is, topics you have a very passionate stance on.

It's All Connected

Practicing emotional regulation is very important because emotions affect all areas of your life. Even though you may not mean to say or do things that are considered rude or inconsiderate, that does not mean you are not accountable for what happens as a result. You have to take responsibility for the things you say and do, fix what you can, and try to respond differently next time.

Our moods, or emotional states, and behaviors are connected. If we feel happy, we are likely to display more positive behaviors, such as smiling, which can lead to feeling happier. Similarly, when we are upset or irritable, we are more likely to avoid social interactions or engage in behaviors that don't serve our best interests, such as buying expensive items we don't need or can't afford.

Learning to recognize and be more aware of the connection between moods and behaviors can lead to more mindful actions and balanced moods over time, as well as lower your level of stress. Use the following chart to write down a few events from your day that you remember well. Fill in what happened, what your response was, and what you could have done differently to make the event more tolerable. Use your findings to determine what you can change, so your future actions align with more positive feelings and emotions. The first row includes sample text as examples to get you started.

TIME AND MOOD BEFORE	WHAT HAPPENED	MY ACTION	IMPACT/ OUTCOME	WHAT CAN I DO NEXT TIME/ OUTCOME?
After work, 6 p.m., grocery store checkout line Stressed, irritable	Person cut in when I was next for checkout	Confronted the person, yelled at them, and used some foul language	People stared at me, were startled, and looked scared I felt good before I looked up, but then I saw red and kept doing the same thing I feel horrible	See all the facts Let it go Move to another line Choose a less busy time to go Would feel fine and not more negative

TIME AND MOOD BEFORE	WHAT HAPPENED	MY ACTION	IMPACT/ OUTCOME	WHAT CAN I DO NEXT TIME/ OUTCOME?

Additional Strategies

- **PUT SOCIAL EVENTS ON YOUR CALENDAR:** Staying engaged with other people is important. Socializing with others will help you feel and know you are connected to something bigger than yourself. But remember, you have to schedule your social plans just like you schedule your work activities.

- **MAKE TIME IN YOUR DAY TO DO WHAT YOU LOVE:** Plan your day with care so you build in time for transitions, and time for people you care about and things you love doing. This will keep you balanced and your mood and morale positive.

- **FORGIVE YOURSELF:** When you start to feel guilt or shame about something that happened in the past, thinking about it constantly or worrying that it will happen again does not help make things better. Instead, observe the thought, and without wishing for it to be different, bring yourself into the present moment by reminding yourself, "I chose to focus on the present because that is what I have control over right now."

- **PRACTICE MINDFUL MOVEMENT ACTIVITIES:** Doing mindfulness activities will help you focus, learn to control your emotions with more intention, and accept yourself as you are and others as they are. Such activities can include yoga, tai chi, dance, working out with weights (while tuning into your breath), running, hiking, bike riding, or anything active that you enjoy. Being outdoors and spending time in nature has a very positive impact on individuals with ADHD.

- **KNOW YOURSELF:** Know your strengths and limitations, as well as the environments, projects, people, and tasks that make you feel successful and productive. On the flip side, know where, what, and who makes you feel awful and ineffective.

A Mindful Heart

Practicing mindfulness has been shown to lead to positive changes in the brains of people who do it consistently for at least two to three months. Mindfulness can help you think clearly, manage stress and moods better, respond instead of react, be more compassionate, and have more positive social interactions.

There are many different mindfulness techniques. For example, when you have a meal, take time to really notice how the food smells, looks, tastes, and feels in your mouth. When you are on a hike or taking a walk, use your senses to explore what you see and hear, or simply enjoy being in nature. When you are in the shower, notice the hot water and how it feels on your neck, hair, and face, and just *be*.

Here's a mindful breathing exercise you can try. Take a deep breath through your nose as you count to five. Hold the breath for two seconds, then slowly exhale for five seconds through your nose. Do this for a minute a few times each day. Notice the sensations in your body as you do it, or how your body feels before and after. You can do this exercise sitting down or even while walking around your house, strolling through the park, or hiking on a trail. After completing this exercise, reflect on your experience below.

_____

_____

_____

_____

_____

_____

_____

_____

Key Takeaways

In this chapter, you have learned about strategies you can add to your ADHD toolkit to help you get more organized, manage your time better, and regulate your emotions to support the positive outcomes you want. The following are some additional suggestions for things you can try to incorporate into your life on a consistent basis.

- If you are planning to do something tomorrow, do it today instead, or even better, do it now. Think of one thing you have been meaning to do but haven't done yet, like doing the laundry or replying to an email you received a few days ago. Do it now!

- Continue to reflect on your strengths and challenges more intentionally. Start your day with hope instead of dread, or acceptance instead of resistance if there is not much you can do to change a situation.

- Challenge every negative thought you have and check what "facts" you used to decide that "everything will always suck" or "my boss doesn't like me and was waiting for me to mess up." Ask yourself, "What facts support this thought?"

- Write a letter to yourself about what you want your life to be like moving forward, starting today, so that when you look back on your life you won't feel regret or guilt.

- Place a sign above your bed that says, "You did your best today. I am proud of you."

I am grateful for the opportunities that each day brings.

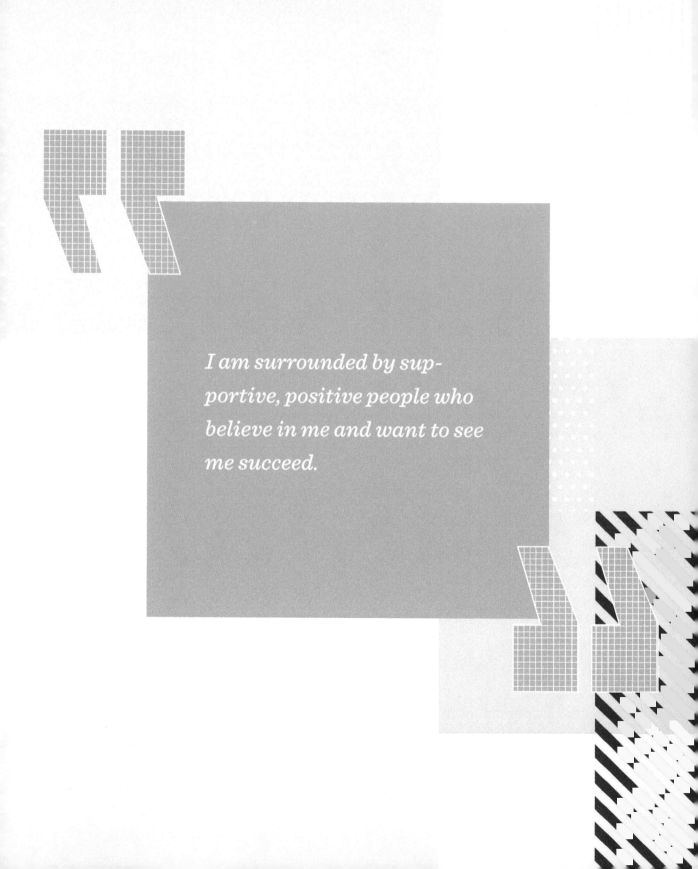

I am surrounded by supportive, positive people who believe in me and want to see me succeed.

CHAPTER 5

Set Yourself Up for Success

L iving a successful life—based on our personal definition of success—is one of the most important goals we set for ourselves. This goal is usually part of the answer to the question "What do I want in life?" Although what success looks like varies from person to person, for an individual with a chronic and complex disorder with many factors to consider, securing help and support from friends, family, and professionals is essential to setting yourself up for success.

Everyone needs help—from getting financial advice to keeping in-boxes and living spaces clutter-free—to ease the stress of the demanding world we live in. This chapter highlights the importance of recognizing when you need help and how to access support from friends, family, and mental health professionals to help you reach your desired outcomes. ADHD affects various areas of your life, and there will be times when you will benefit from summoning the courage to ask for help.

For individuals with ADHD, being part of social groups or communities and staying connected with others is especially important. You will have the opportunity to meet others with similar challenges and learn how they manage their ADHD symptoms. Additionally, you will have a group of people who collectively will be able to provide you with the specific resources and referrals you need. Asking for help means opening yourself to improved well-being, but often unhelpful advice can bring up feelings of shame or frustration. Though that may happen, the feelings will pass as soon as you see the positive responses from those around you who are willing to support you. If you feel stressed and overwhelmed by the idea of reaching out for help, remind yourself that these are normal responses to change and will quickly pass. The activities in this chapter will help you find and practice the best way for you to feel comfortable and empowered when asking for help.

NEO'S STORY

Neo found himself looking through stacks of paper on his desk and the floor of his room in an effort to find an important document. He couldn't remember where he put it and didn't want to ask his parents out of fear that they would remind him how disorganized he was. So, he kept looking, and before he knew it, it had been an hour and he was late for dinner plans with his friends. By the time he got to the restaurant, his friends barely greeted him and made a joke about how late he always was. Neo explained what was going on with him and said that he needed support with getting things together and organized. His friends expressed empathy and one of them even shared that he was diagnosed with ADHD and had had similar challenges before getting supports in place. Neo felt a lot better after hearing that and got some good referrals from this friend. All of his friends were encouraging and acknowledged his struggles. They also offered to help Neo—without judgment—if he asked.

Getting Comfortable Asking for Help

If asking for help is difficult for you, don't worry, you aren't alone. Many people are uncomfortable asking for help because it can bring up unpleasant feelings such as incompetence, dependence on others, or irresponsibility. Working to identify what makes you feel uncomfortable with asking for the help you need, and then taking small steps toward accepting the idea of asking for help as a normal action, is essential for a successful life. Over the years, you have probably had some bad experiences when you asked for help—from family, friends, teachers, colleagues, or bosses—causing you to feel embarrassed or ashamed. The frustration of missing deadlines and appointments or struggling with assignments and instructions could certainly impact how you see yourself and make you more self-conscious. These feelings and emotions may be experienced and responded to more intensely than necessary because of the ADHD brain's circuitry and chemicals. Although this automatic thought and action pattern can impact important relationships in all areas of your life, it can be redirected and used to work for you and not against you. This won't happen overnight, and that news may sound frustrating. However, taking small, conscious, and consistent steps in the short term can make a noticeable impact and lead to significant changes in the long term.

For a variety of reasons, many men with ADHD will endure difficult feelings and consequences without verbalizing their situation. Social messages stigmatize mental health in general, so there is a fear of disclosing personal information because it may affect their career and relationships. Here is the reality: Asking for help is an act of courage and vulnerability. Being vulnerable is a positive sign, because it means you understand that you are struggling and are willing to put yourself out there. Sharing your challenges with time management and attention, for example, can help provide a starting point to help you and your partner work toward saving your relationship. Proactively telling your friends about the struggles you have with initiating plans and why you chronically cancel or show up late to things could save your friendships and even make them stronger. Many people don't want to ask for help because they feel they will be a burden on others, but that is only a thought, not a fact. The ADHD mind is very persuasive when it comes to talking you out of things. To counter that, think about it as being proactive in your process of change. Try to take control of a situation and put supports in place before the situation gets worse.

Asking for help during a difficult time is a sign of maturity, wisdom, and self-awareness. We all need help from time to time—working together is what brought us all this far. Remind yourself that humans are a social species, and asking others for help for yourself is no different from the times you offered your help to others—without judgment. Think of the feelings you had for someone who was struggling and how you didn't hesitate to help. Maybe now it's time for you to be the one to be helped, and maybe that same person gets the chance to be the helper. There is no shame in knowing your limits and respecting yourself enough to find ways to be more effective, efficient, and successful in all areas of your life.

Today, technology makes it easier to connect with others in similar circumstances. There are many professionals out there who can assist you—from those who can help you get your living space and schedule organized, to doctors and therapists who can work with you to figure out a treatment plan that works for you. If seeking help is hard for you, think about the impact of not getting the support you need in all aspects of your life. Open your heart and allow yourself to see the power of connection when you receive the help you need. Someday, you might be able to help someone else.

What Do I Need?

For many men, asking for help can bring up feelings of vulnerability, embarrassment, and frustration. The feelings that show up are connected to the messages you received during your childhood and adulthood about asking for help, and the responses you received. The goals of this activity are to encourage you to explore the barriers that prevent you from seeking support from others when you need it, and empower you to figure out what you need help with and how you can seek out that help.

1. Turn on some soothing music and get into a comfortable sitting or lying position.

2. Hold a smooth rock or stress ball in each hand. You can use them as fidgets if that is helpful.

3. Close your eyes and take a deep breath while counting to five. Hold the breath for two counts, then breathe out for seven counts.

4. Imagine watching yourself as a child, playing on a playground or with a toy in your room.

5. Now observe yourself falling from a swing or struggling with your toy and asking your parents or others around you for help.

6. Stay with the image and notice how you feel, along with any sensations you are having in your body.

7. What happens next? Do you get the help you need? If not, what happens instead?

8. Stay with what you notice and simply observe without trying to change anything.

9. Come back to your breath and focus on it as you open your eyes and come back to the present moment.

In the space provided, write down what you remember about a time you needed help. Did you ask for help, wait for it, or keep going without it? What did you learn about yourself regarding asking for help?

When Going It Alone Doesn't Cut It

Picking up from the last exercise, this section will further focus on your getting the help you need and how you can do that. Trying to deal with the challenges of ADHD alone can make things more difficult and end up working against you. The same parts of your brain that help you concentrate are the same parts that work to help you manage your emotions and regulate all your actions. So, when you are stressed, your ability to concentrate, stay organized, and manage your emotional responses can feel even more impaired. But things don't have to be this way, and you don't have to go through this alone. Getting help and support can relieve some of the burden you have been carrying and finally allow you see what you are capable of. If asking people you know for referrals or recommendations isn't for you, technology offers alternative ways to find the support you need. Refer to the Resources section at the end of this workbook (see page 121) for more details about options that may be helpful to you.

That said, the best resources often come from the people you know personally and trust most. This is where opening your heart and trusting others to come through for you during a difficult time can prove to be an empowering and humbling experience. Connecting with other people who are going through similar challenges can be therapeutic in its own way, and can help remind you that there are others out there who are going through similar difficulties. It may sound hard, and it is, but allowing your loved ones—friends or family—into your life as part of your support system can make a positive impact on your life and give you the boost in self-confidence you deserve.

BLAKE'S STORY

Blake was struggling to keep his appointments, was constantly late picking up his children at school, and often forgot to refill important prescriptions for his elderly parents, who relied on him for help. Between his obligations at work and at home, Blake was increasingly distracted, stressed, and irritable. At work, Blake often rushed from one meeting to another without leaving enough time to eat a proper lunch or take a quick walk to offset the long hours sitting at a desk. By the end of his workday, Blake was completely exhausted—emotionally, mentally, and physically. Blake's partner was getting very upset and starting to feel like a single parent, taking care of the entire household's responsibilities while also working full time. Blake found himself constantly apologizing to everyone in his life for being late, forgetting important events, or being irritable and yelling. He knew something wasn't right, but was worried that telling his partner would make it sound like he was coming up with new excuses. Knowing something had to change, he found a website for a local advocacy group for adult ADHD and reached out to a few mental health professionals who were listed for consultations. With the right support and guidance in place, he wanted to tell his friends and family about his struggles.

Talking to Friends

Talking to friends about your challenges can be understandably uncomfortable. But avoiding the conversation with people you value and want in your life is like taking off a bandage really, really slowly—so slowly that you realize the wound is now infected because you kept the bandage on for too long. Maintaining social interactions and positive relationships is important because your friends can provide stress relief, companionship, and support when you need to speak with someone. Unfortunately, emotional impulsivity and dysregulation can result in angry outbursts toward friends due to misinterpretations of their gestures, forgetting important events in their lives, or perhaps drinking too much and getting into an altercation with them verbally or physically. Such behavior can cause rifts and bruising in your friendships. However, keep in mind that bruises heal—some take longer than others, but they do heal. Use the strategies listed here to help you have meaningful and honest conversations with your friends about the ways your ADHD symptoms manifest themselves and how they impact your life.

- Have an honest, authentic, and heartfelt conversation about what adult ADHD is and how it affects you specifically, including your ability to concentrate, get organized, and regulate your emotions and moods.

- Give your friend a fact sheet with information about adult ADHD.

- Choose a time when you are least likely to be stressed and can allow yourself to listen and respond—not react—to any feedback you receive.

- Lead with specific situations where symptoms of ADHD, such as impulsivity or emotional dysregulation, led to you saying things you didn't mean or an escalated situation where you took things personally when they weren't aimed at you in any way. Then genuinely state:

  - "I felt terrible after I said that, and I knew right away I went too far," or, "My brain doesn't always hit the brakes fast enough between thinking and doing."

  - Emphasize that you are not making excuses, but just offering explanations to give some context regarding the medical condition affecting you.

- Let your friends ask questions. Share what you are comfortable talking about. Ask if they can help keep you accountable as you work toward your desired outcomes—one being maintaining your friendship with them.

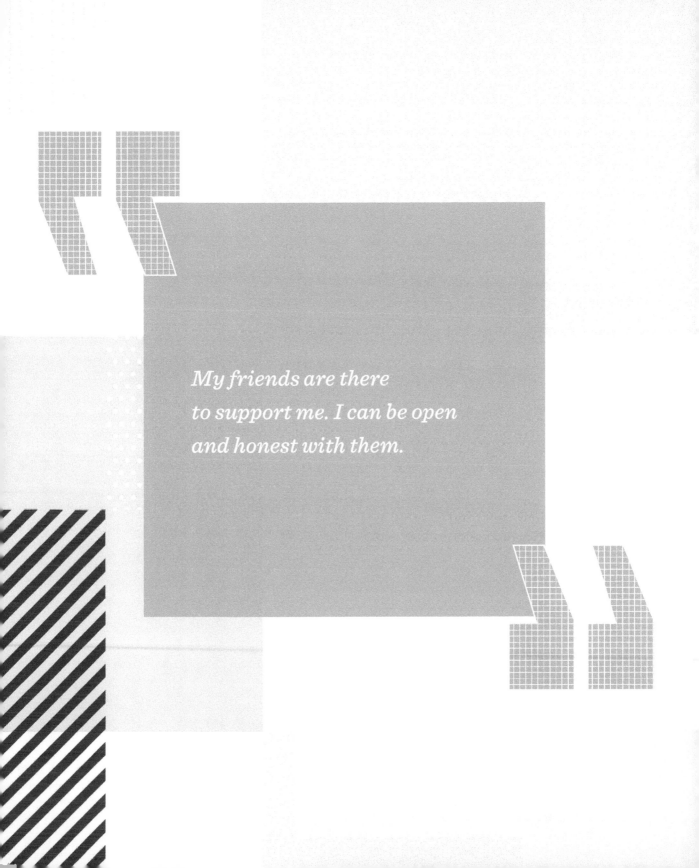

*My friends are there
to support me. I can be open
and honest with them.*

Describe, Decide, Visualize, and Practice

It can be helpful to practice coping with difficult situations ahead of time, as this leads to better emotional regulation and overall self-control. Use the following exercise to help you practice this skill.

DESCRIBE
how you think it will go (who you will talk to, what about, why, when, where, and anticipated emotional and verbal responses).

DECIDE
what you will do to manage impulsivity and emotional dysregulation.

VISUALIZE
yourself in the situation right now.

PRACTICE
what you will say and do, and practice coping with the worst anticipated outcomes. Practice relaxation after.

Think of a hypothetical scenario that you would find difficult to cope with. Write your responses to each of the previously listed steps in the spaces provided.

DESCRIBE:

_____

_____

_____

_____

_____

_____

_____

DECIDE:

_____

_____

_____

_____

_____

_____

PRACTICE:

How do you feel after practicing what you will say and do, visualizing yourself in the situation, and preparing for the worst anticipated outcomes? How do you feel practicing relaxation after?

_____

_____

_____

_____

_____

_____

_____

_____

Talking to Colleagues (Especially Your Boss)

The complex nature of ADHD, along with the variety of symptoms different people express and the lack of awareness regarding adult ADHD symptoms, are a few of the reasons why deciding whether to disclose the diagnosis at work can be difficult. General societal stigmas attached to mental health disorders and fear of being fired or overlooked for promotions only make this sensitive decision even more difficult. That said, it can be very empowering, freeing, and human to be vulnerable and open about being diagnosed with ADHD and how it affects you. Keep in mind that your boss and colleagues can't help you if they don't know what you are struggling with and what you need to be successful at work. Also remember that it's in the best interest of your boss and company to support you because your success means their success.

Use the following strategies to help you prepare for the conversation with your boss. Before you have this conversation, make sure you are aware of the laws in your state, as well as the company's culture. Also consider your comfort level with your boss. Meeting with your human resources (HR) representative in confidence may be a good place to start, since they can clarify the process and your options, and help facilitate the conversation between you and your boss, if needed. In some cases, using the benefits available through the Family Medical Leave Act, especially if you need extended time off, may be a better route.

1. Think about why you're disclosing this information in the first place. What support do you need? It's best to refrain from talking with your boss until you have clarity about what you are looking for. Once you are clear about the changes you need, go to HR first and document your meeting with them—the time and date, what was discussed, who was there, and the resolutions reached. In most cases, HR should be able to help you put together a plan of action you can discuss with your boss.

2. Before you speak to your boss, tell a colleague you are on friendly terms with and welcome any insights they may have to help you determine the best course of action within the context of the company's culture.

3. The company's work culture and your relationship with your boss will determine the best way for you to have this conversation. If you have a new boss or the company culture is somewhat formal, request a meeting through email and suggest a time when things are less busy at work. If it's a more casual environment, you may ask your boss to grab a coffee with you or go for a walk and talk outdoors. Make sure to keep your conversation professional and focused on how ADHD is impacting you at work and explain what supports you think you need.

DO YOU NEED TO INVOLVE HR?

ADHD is a condition that requires companies to offer reasonable accommodations to employees so that they can do their jobs without it adversely affecting their mental health. Under the Americans with Disabilities Act (ADA), you can ask for modifications, such as a change in work hours, use of headphones to help with distractions, and a change in desk placement or even lighting. Any adjustments that will require time off or a change to your work hours or schedule are best handled by going through HR. You don't have to explicitly tell HR that you have ADHD, but it would be advised in situations where your symptoms are causing functional impairments—meaning the disorder is impacting your quality of life and affecting your ability to do your job at the level that is expected. Once you go to HR, know that your requests will be documented, and the HR representative may ask for a letter from your therapist or doctor to confirm the challenges or diagnosis. You do not have to submit anything, because a diagnosis is part of your medical record and therefore you have a right to keep it confidential; however, providing a letter of support or recommendations from a clinician who can speak to your specific needs and offer solutions will benefit you. For example, if daily reprimands for tardiness, careless mistakes, and emotional outbursts affect your work, they are causing a functional impairment and require that your company provide you with appropriate and reasonable accommodations under ADA. Most accommodations are inexpensive and can be provided with existing resources in the office.

Think It Through

A perceived fear of rejection, ridicule, or discrimination can make it tough to decide whether you should disclose your ADHD diagnosis to your colleagues and boss at work. On the other hand, disclosing the diagnosis and explaining your needs might bring you relief. Take your time and think through your decision. Fill in the following boxes to help you determine what will work best for you. Then complete the following section.

	Pros	Cons
Disclose		
Do Not Disclose		

Having thought this through, I have decided that it's in my best interest to [ ] disclose [ ] not disclose my ADHD diagnosis to my colleagues, my boss, or HR at this time because . . .

....

....

....

I can always ask ...., my ....

...., to help me if I am not sure about what to do.

Talking to Family

An adult diagnosis of ADHD can often lead to the discovery that parents and siblings also have ADHD that has been undiagnosed or untreated due to cultural, social, or religious reasons. Revealing your diagnosis to your family may generate an authentic conversation with your parents and siblings about your family history and dynamics, while also encouraging them to seek evaluations if ADHD-related symptoms and/or patterns of behavior are present. Use the following strategies to begin the process of having a conversation with your parents, siblings, and partner.

1. Depending on your parents' ages, cultural expectations, and needs, you can engage in a conversation with them about your diagnosis by expressing the challenges you are having that led you to see your doctor and the process leading up to your ADHD diagnosis. Use facts that you received from your doctor, including how ADHD has a strong genetic influence, meaning that if a child has it, one or both parents are likely to have ADHD. Help them explore the benefits of receiving an ADHD diagnosis and what medical treatment could mean for them at their age. It could mean treatment to alleviate symptoms that are serving as barriers to being more independent, or access to more support through their insurance or state benefits. Keep in mind that it may be hard for your parents to understand or accept the diagnosis now, so if they are unable to engage further, leave it at sharing your experience and what you need them to help you with.

2. Revealing your ADHD diagnosis can serve as a starting point for sincere conversations between you and your partner as you work toward making amends for complex interactions. Emphasize you are not looking to be excused for your actions, but rather use these conversations as an opportunity to provide an explanation for the specific challenges in your relationship and to accept accountability for your actions going forward. Assessing, acknowledging, and accepting your relationship dynamics as they are and finding common ground to develop a true partnership provides a beginning to the healing process—whatever the eventual outcome may be.

3. Offer your partner a concrete written plan describing what chores you can take on to make the distribution more equal and when you plan to do those chores. Be proactive in planning social gatherings, family trips, and activities with your children. In your written plan, include dates and times alongside your ideas to demonstrate your commitment to improving your organizational skills and overall engagement with the family. Keep the plan and/or calendar visible, and empower your partner to hold you accountable should you forget something or need a gentle reminder.

Talking to Children about Your ADHD

Talking to children in your life about ADHD may seem difficult to do; however, it can be an opportunity for you to have an authentic and honest interaction with them. With the increase in diagnoses and information regarding ADHD, chances are most children are probably aware of a classmate or friend with the condition. Speaking to them about the challenges that come with ADHD can be an opportunity to debunk any myths they may have heard and instill a sense of empathy for their peers who are struggling with ADHD. Furthermore, you can use this conversation to discuss neurodivergence in general, providing a perspective that nurtures the idea of celebrating and embracing individual differences and abilities. Providing information in an age-appropriate way is important. For younger children, it's best to use a storybook with characters who discuss neurodivergence or individual differences. This will make it easier for the child to relate to the information.

Here are some additional tips for talking about your ADHD with children:

- The child may know a classmate or friend who has ADHD, so adjust the information according to the child's age and knowledge base.

- Talk about the strengths you have and highlight them. (For instance, if the child is young, you could say, "The great thing is that it gives me so much energy to play with you.")

- Be honest and answer any questions they have (as appropriate for their age).

- Emphasize that ADHD isn't about being odd or different in a bad way, but rather that it just means being different. Period. You do things differently from other adults at times, and even though you may be late or forget things because you are distracted, you also have lots of great qualities like creativity.

- Use jokes or humor when you can to keep the conversation light.

Talk It Out

For this exercise, you will examine the barriers you may experience when speaking with your family members about ADHD, and brainstorm ways that you can help make the conversation easier.

Work your way up the pyramid, recording one barrier in each level according to the difficulty level of the issue. Then write down possible solutions to these barriers in the lines provided.

For example:

Barrier 1 (lowest level): Generation or cultural gap between myself and parents.

Possible solution: Ask family members they respect to highlight how getting help for a health issue was useful.

BARRIERS:

3: ....

2: ....

1: ....

POSSIBLE SOLUTIONS:

Barrier 1: ....

Barrier 2: ....

Barrier 3: ....

Key Takeaways

This chapter emphasized the importance of being open to asking for help and accessing the different resources available to you, at home and at work, to set yourself up for success. Although asking for help may bring up unpleasant feelings, exploring the underlying reasons that prevent you from seeking help is an important first step. A variety of resources and remedies are available to you—including mental health professionals, accommodations at work, and organizational consultants—to help you be your most effective self. Of course, support from friends and family is priceless and can go a long way. When things feel overwhelming, remind yourself to breathe, assess what you need, and follow up by creating a plan. The wonderful thing about acknowledging you need help is the relief that follows when you receive it. Self-acceptance, self-compassion, and embracing the fact that everybody needs help with something—and knowing you will have an opportunity to help others at some point—can lead to positive improvements in your professional and personal life.

- Make a list of things you need help with and think about who you know personally whom you can reach out to for help.

- Find two online resources that can provide the help you need.

- At work, identify who the disability coordinator or designated HR representative is and confidentially meet with them to request workplace accommodations when you need the support.

- Using the strategies provided in this chapter, practice speaking about your ADHD diagnosis with your friends and family.

- Remember to give yourself credit for taking the leap and asking for help—it is not an easy thing to do! Plan some rewarding activities for yourself during the week.

I see asking for help as a sign of maturity and wisdom. I will ask for help for the things I don't know, as asking for help is a way to expand my connections. I will thank those who helped me, take credit for stepping out of my comfort zone, smile, and remember the positive outcome.

To live a life that is in alignment with my goals and values, I choose to begin by doing things differently, starting with making small lifestyle changes daily—because I can't be who I want to be by doing the things I used to do.

CHAPTER 6

Managing ADHD with Lifestyle Changes

Having ADHD is nothing to be ashamed of. However, the disorder does require professional help to manage the various ways in which the symptoms impact your life. This chapter will explore different types of professional help available (medical and nonmedical), when seeking therapy should become a priority, and discuss holistic interventions and strategies that promote positive lifestyle choices. A comprehensive treatment plan for adults with ADHD may include all or some of the following components:

- Medication (stimulant and/or nonstimulant)
- Cognitive behavioral therapy
- Lifestyle changes to address sleep, exercise, diet, and stress
- Strategies to develop structure, consistency, and accountability

- Meditation, yoga, dance, and sports activities to improve mood and reduce hyperactivity

- Practicing skills in session

- Vitamins and supplements, as directed by a doctor

- Follow-ups with other professionals to coordinate effective care

- ADHD group therapy or support groups

- Occasional family or couples sessions

- Strengths-based, inclusive, and culturally sensitive approaches

- Increase of adaptive thinking processes

An analysis of the different medications used to treat adult ADHD and their characteristics is also included in this chapter.

Since practice makes progress, a variety of exercises are offered that you can start using right away. Although monitoring your behaviors is essential to achieving positive treatment outcomes, addressing lifestyle issues that make ADHD symptoms more likely to surface—such as poor sleep, poor diet, lack of exercise, unanticipated changes in routines, and substance use or misuse—is equally important. Although using the strategies and exercises in this workbook can provide you with an amazing start toward managing your symptoms of ADHD, it's crucial that you consult your medical doctor or a licensed medical professional with expertise in treating adult ADHD before implementing any lifestyle or medication changes. If you are feeling impatient, use that feeling as motivation to schedule an appointment with your doctor today to discuss your plan and follow their recommendations.

KAI'S STORY

Kai was able to contact a psychiatrist that a friend recommended for a medication consultation. Kai had some hesitation and anxiety about becoming dependent on medication that he might have to take for the rest of his life. Upon meeting with the psychiatrist, Kai was honest about his resistance to medication and feeling overwhelmed by the idea. After a thorough evaluation, including taking an inventory of Kai's symptoms, his developmental history, and other medications being taken, the psychiatrist explained the different options that would be well suited to Kai, explored Kai's questions, and offered different perspectives that helped Kai determine that medication was the right choice for him. The psychiatrist suggested starting stimulant medications and cautioned Kai that they would need to do trials with a few medications over the next month to see which worked best for him. In addition to addressing ADHD, the psychiatrist suggested Wellbutrin, a serotonin-norepinephrine reuptake inhibitor (SNRI), to treat Kai's symptoms of depression. The psychiatrist also recommended individual behavioral therapy to practice the skills needed to improve executive function deficits and process the emotional challenges presented by ADHD. Once the right medications and dosages were determined, Kai noticed significant changes in his mood and concentration, and decreases in hyperactivity and anxiety. He felt hopeful and ready to plan the rest of his life, moving forward with excitement instead of doubt for the first time.

Professional Support

Anyone may experience depression or anxiety from time to time. These feelings become a disorder when the symptoms start to interfere with your life in negative ways, causing impairments in your ability to function and participate in your daily responsibilities at work, at home, and in social situations. If this happens, it is a good idea to seek professional help from a therapist or doctor with expertise in diagnosing and treating adult ADHD and its coexisting conditions, such as clinical depression, substance abuse disorders, generalized anxiety or borderline personality disorder, or obsessive-compulsive disorder. You may be concerned about finding a therapist or doctor with expertise in diagnosing and treating adult ADHD, and that is a valid concern. There are many types of health care professionals who are licensed to diagnose and treat ADHD, often causing confusion and delay in selecting the correct provider.

Due to the complex nature of ADHD, it is difficult to diagnose. Regardless of the clinician's license, it is imperative that you seek help from a clinician who focuses on serving the adult population with ADHD, has a significant amount of training and experience working with adults with ADHD and/or related disorders, and is willing to collaborate with other professionals helping you, making you feel heard and supported. The therapeutic relationship can have a pivotal impact on positive treatment outcomes.

As previously discussed, one of the reasons getting an ADHD diagnosis is important is because it allows you access to the effective treatments available. A thorough treatment plan includes the use of medications to treat the symptoms of ADHD, along with medications to treat coexisting disorders—such as depression and anxiety—that are likely to be present. Most adults who decide to use medication as part of their treatment plan for ADHD report feeling like they are on the same playing field as their peers for the first time in their lives.

When to Seek Therapy

Although you can seek professional help anytime, you're the expert on yourself, so trust your instincts as to when you believe your symptoms are adversely affecting your life. Adult ADHD has some complex symptoms, and these can be displayed to different degrees. The level of impairment the symptoms pose in your personal and professional lives is categorized as mild, medium, or severe.

Here are a few general guidelines and benefits regarding seeking professional help:

- A clinician specializing in ADHD will help make sure that your symptoms aren't being caused by a condition other than ADHD that requires attention.

- Therapy, starting with a diagnostic evaluation, is necessary in order to get a prescription for stimulant medications, which are highly effective first-line treatments for ADHD and symptom management.

- Therapy sessions will help you discern your strengths and weaknesses, so you can direct your coping efforts to the areas where they're needed.

- The best ways to find licensed health care providers with expertise in diagnosing and treating adult ADHD is through referrals from people you know; your insurance company's member services department; online therapist directories such as those provided by *Psychology Today*, Monarch, or Headway; and/or apps like Inflow.

- Online therapist directories are good resources for scheduling a medication consultation or an initial diagnostic assessment for ADHD with a psychiatrist, neurologist, psychiatric nurse practitioner, or physician's assistant.

- It's not unusual to meet with more than one therapist, especially if you didn't feel a connection to the first one. But sometimes it's important to give a therapist a second try—your initial reaction could be the result of your own resistance to seeking therapy, which is a very normal occurrence. Remind yourself that it's a new experience that will take a while to get comfortable with, especially if you are completely new to the therapeutic process. Hang in there! Having a strong therapeutic rapport with your therapist is essential for successful treatment outcomes.

When to Seek Medication

If you have a history of being treated for depression or anxiety with a class of medications referred to as selective serotonin reuptake inhibitors (or SSRIs), such as Zoloft or Lexapro, and have not seen any improvement, have had adverse reactions, or have even seen symptoms get worse, that is likely a clue that you have ADHD, not depression or anxiety. When ADHD is treated with medications, it is common to see positive improvements in symptoms of depression and anxiety as well. If you are considering trying medication to treat your symptoms of ADHD, it's best to get properly evaluated by a professional with experience treating adult ADHD. It is important to note that if you do plan to use medication, you should speak with your doctor regarding the substances you use, including caffeine and nicotine. Drinking excessive amounts of coffee while taking a stimulant medication can cause rapid heart rate, dry mouth, and increased anxiety levels.

The medications used to treat ADHD are highly controlled substances. Clinical trials to examine the effects of approved medications are performed using a few different medications to find those that work the best. The dosage varies based on the body's response to the medication, but the FDA has established maximum dosages for therapeutic use. Most doctors aim to use the lowest amount of the medication that effectively provides symptom relief.

STIMULANTS
BRAND NAME(S): Adderall, Dexedrine, Ritalin, Vyvanse, Concerta
BASIC INFORMATION: Comes in instant-release and extended- or slow-release formulas. Effects last while the dose is in your system, anywhere from 3 to 5 hours for immediate-release and 8 to 12 hours for extended release-formulas. Some unpleasant side effects include loss of appetite, increased heart rate, increased thirst, insomnia, headaches, and muscle tension.

NON-STIMULANTS

BRAND NAME(S): Strattera

BASIC INFORMATION: The only FDA-approved nonstimulant medication used for ADHD. It works similarly to the way stimulants work. It will take four to six weeks for you to fully feel the effects, and you have to taper back down to the lowest dosage if you want to stop. It's effective and useful, especially with other medical conditions that prohibit use of stimulant medications. It will take longer than stimulant medication to determine effective therapeutic dosage.

It's reported to not be as effective as stimulants. Other medications such as SNRIs are used in tandem.

SEROTONIN-NOREPINEPHRINE REUPTAKE INHIBITOR (SNRI)

BRAND NAME(S): Cymbalta, Wellbutrin

BASIC INFORMATION: Effective in treating symptoms of depression and anxiety disorders, along with symptoms of mild ADHD. People with ADHD often respond to SNRIs better than SSRIs like Zoloft or Lexapro, because SNRIs address deficient levels of brain chemicals such as dopamine and norepinephrine, as opposed to serotonin alone. It can take three to six weeks to fully experience the medication's effects and effective dose. The lowest dosage is typically increased every two to three weeks until the optimal dosage is found. Side effects include loss of appetite, headaches, weight gain, and withdrawal effects if large doses are abruptly stopped. You must taper the medication under the supervision and guidance of your doctor.

Lifestyle Inventory

Complete this inventory by filling in information about your current lifestyle habits, such as how much sleep you get, what you do for exercise, what you eat, and so on. You can use this information to determine and/or reflect on whether making lifestyle changes would be useful for you, and if so, in what areas. Additionally, you can share this information with your health care provider.

SLEEP (e.g., 8 to 10 hours nightly, same sleep/wake time, sleep through the night)	
EXERCISE (e.g., 20 to 30 minutes/day, yoga, tai chi, cardio, dance, walking)	
DIET AND NUTRITION (e.g., eat three meals a day; eat healthy snacks, if needed, high in protein, low in sugar and carbs; take vitamins and supplements, if needed)	
STRESS MANAGEMENT (e.g., meditation, effective scheduling, mindfulness and breathing exercises)	
MOODS (e.g., irritable, happy, frazzled, sad, anxious)	
OTHER LIFESTYLE ISSUES	

Cutting Out ADHD Triggers

In addition to medication and behavioral therapy, there are lifestyle changes you can make to manage ADHD proactively and maximize the positive effects of your treatment. Getting enough sleep, eating healthy foods, exercising for at least 30 minutes a day, and managing daily stress levels are all lifestyle habits that facilitate a balanced and healthier mind and body, in turn lowering the severity of ADHD symptoms and their impact on your personal and professional lives. More often than not, a good day begins the night before. What this means is that poor sleep (time and quality) the night before an important presentation is likely to make you feel more irritable, anxious, and fatigued the day of your presentation, potentially leading to errors and forgetfulness. Remember, these behaviors do not mean you are incompetent or unintelligent. Rather, they underscore the importance of developing and following a daily routine of getting seven to nine hours of sleep a night; eating high-protein and iron-rich foods; and (ideally) eliminating sugars, caffeine, and alcohol, or decreasing their intake.

There are many complementary and alternative medicine (CAM) techniques that can be incorporated into your treatment plan. These interventions include Eastern and ancient practices from various cultures—such as breath work, yoga, tai chi, chanting or meditation, acupuncture, mindfulness practices, and the use of vitamins and supplements to address mineral deficiencies in your body—to address ADHD symptoms.

Lifestyle changes and modifications can allow you to better manage stress in your personal and professional lives, and lower levels of stress can mean better health, a more balanced emotional state, proactive planning or problem-solving, and a happier life. Of course, consult your health care provider before you make any changes to your treatment plan or take any supplements.

COREY'S STORY

Corey benefited from seeing a health care provider with an expertise in ADHD, and together they created a treatment plan that worked well for him. The plan included stimulant medication for ADHD symptoms; SNRI antidepressant medication to address depression; supplements to address vitamin deficiencies; meditation, yoga, and acupuncture to aid in stress management; cutting out alcohol and excessive caffeine consumption; and eating nutritious meals rich in protein. Immediately after starting the stimulant medication that worked for him, Corey experienced a boost in focus and attention that also lowered his anxiety, opening up energy and room to implement the behavioral strategies he learned through consistent behavior therapy with a therapist knowledgeable in ADHD. After four weeks of routinely complying with his comprehensive and holistic treatment plan, Corey saw significant gains—he was less irritable, more socially engaged, kinder to himself, more proactive when it came to work, and he felt more in control of his life. These changes positively improved his interactions with friends and family, which increased his motivation to stick with the changes he was making, even on days when it felt hard. He just focused on the positive feelings he felt when he was following through on his schedule and lifestyle goals.

Stress Management

Stress is part of everyone's life from time to time; however, chronic stress is toxic to the brain and one's overall health and wellness. For adults with ADHD, chronic stress can further compromise the executive functioning skills the brain relies on to get things done, filter information received, and respond appropriately, which impacts key personal and professional relationships. Not all stress is bad stress, however. Some examples of "good" stress include starting a new job, starting your own business, or becoming a parent for the first time. Because these events are generally perceived as positive, the impact of the stress may be experienced in a less toxic way by your mind and body. Keep in mind that everyone's tolerance for stress is different; therefore, don't minimize your struggles because they may seem insignificant compared to someone else's, or because coworkers or classmates aren't reporting the same amount of stress. What impacts you is what matters.

Chronic stress is often the result of having poor coping skills, a negative thought pattern that automatically jumps to the worst-case scenario, chaotic environments at home or work due to poor organizational and time management skills, working memory challenges, and emotional dysregulation. Over time, the increased amounts of stress hormones, such as cortisol, released by your brain can lead to weight disturbances, an increase or decrease in appetite, premature aging, a decrease in self-care activities, sexual dissatisfaction, fatigue, feeling overwhelmed, and insomnia or poor quality of sleep—all of which worsen ADHD symptoms and adversely impact key personal and professional relationships. Without positive stress management strategies in place, severe depression and anxiety may also occur.

Proactively managing your level of stress can significantly increase positive emotional regulation, decrease distractibility and hyperactivity, and boost task completion and mood. Use the following tips to get your stress under control and live a happier life.

- **NAME IT:** Identify what causes you stress and determine if it's something that is within your control to address or eliminate. It's important to note that not everything is within your control to address; however, focusing on what you *can* control in those situations is often helpful. For example, if you have a test coming up, getting enough rest, eating well, and studying efficiently are all things within your control, but despite the efforts you put in, certainty about the outcome is not within your control. Use any insights you gain to develop a proactive plan to help you change what you can, accept certain truths that you can't change, and proceed from there.

- **PUT IT IN YOUR CALENDAR:** Create a weekly healthy habits or wellness schedule and track your progress by placing a plus sign (you did it) or minus sign (you didn't do it) next to the activity you scheduled on a specific day. The wellness or healthy habits listed should include eating healthy meals; exercising daily using movement-based activities such as running, hiking, yoga, tai chi, dance, and sports; and engaging in mindfulness and meditation practices that you use throughout the week, especially during stressful situations. Practice these techniques in all settings you encounter, not just at home. Give yourself small rewards for following through on them. A reward can be extra TV time, dinner at your favorite restaurant, or buying something you have had your eye on.

- **SCHEDULE TIME IN YOUR DAY FOR WHAT MATTERS:** Make it a habit to have positive experiences daily by engaging in positive activities or things you enjoy doing with people you enjoy being with. Learn to effectively prioritize and manage your time so you can come home earlier from work to enjoy dinner with your family, or take a daily, 20-minute mindful walk to decompress and energize yourself before tackling a big project.

Stress Test

This exercise will give you an opportunity to put the previously listed strategies into practice. You will think about three areas in your life that cause you stress, identify specific stressors that impact you, and list something you can do that is realistic and within your control to address the stress. Make sure to mark the date that you will start using each technique and track your progress.

1. What situation causes me stress? What stressors impact me?

....

....

....

Circle the number that indicates the level of stress experienced.

1   2   3   4   5   6   7   8   9   10

Can I control this? If yes, what I can do about it and when will I start? If no, what can I do to accept the situation?

....

....

....

2. What situation causes me stress? What stressors impact me?

....

....

....

Circle the number that indicates the level of stress experienced.

1   2   3   4   5   6   7   8   9   10

CONTINUED >

Can I control this? If yes, what I can do about it and when will I start? If no, what can I do to accept the situation?

_____

_____

_____

3. What situation causes me stress? What stressors impact me?

_____

_____

_____

Circle the number that indicates the level of stress experienced.

1   2   3   4   5   6   7   8   9   10

Can I control this? If yes, what I can do about it and when will I start? If no, what can I do to accept the situation?

_____

_____

_____

Overscheduling or taking on too much can exacerbate certain ADHD symptoms, such as poor time management skills, lack of self-awareness (at times), planning and organizational skills deficits, and poor working memory, which erases connections to past mistakes made due to scheduling too much, further contributing to overscheduling behaviors and increased stress. All of this can negatively impact overall mind–body functioning. Additionally, many adults with ADHD have people-pleasing tendencies, making it hard for them to say no, which also contributes to overscheduling behaviors.

- **SCHEDULE SMARTLY:** Block off 10 to 15 minutes between meetings or tasks that require sitting for long periods of time and use the time to stretch, walk around, get a high-protein snack, or decompress using breathing exercises. When you begin a task you don't like, start a timer and see how long you are able to focus without losing attention and motivation. See if you can focus for 20 minutes before you lose focus, then work for 20 minutes more, then take a 10-minute brain break. Try to slowly increase the time you can focus on doing something before taking a break. Also try scheduling a "want to do" task after a "have to do" task to increase your motivation to get through a task that needs to get done.

- **SAY "NO" (TACTFULLY):** Learn to decline extra projects, taking on extra work from coworkers, and attending events you don't want to go to. You don't have to provide an explanation, but offer a reply—a brief one is fine. For example, you can say, "Thank you for the invitation, but unfortunately I can't attend" or "I appreciate that you thought of me for this project; however, I am unable to accept new projects due to a full schedule at the moment." This will allow you to focus on what you need to complete and to honor deadlines, because you are in control of your schedule. Taking on commitments to please others at the expense of your mental health is not worth it.

- **BE MINDFUL OF EMOTIONAL TENDENCIES:** You may get excited about starting new things when you are having a good day or moment, only to feel overwhelmed and avoidant of the commitment you signed up for when you are having a difficult time. Before starting something new, like projects or classes, look into the time commitment required and expectations to be met, check your schedule to assess the feasibility of committing to the project or class, and then decide whether you will go ahead with it or pass. Of course, unexpected changes can disrupt your schedule or planning efforts, and that is why it's so important to leave openings in your schedule for downtime, which provide the flexibility to reschedule something, if needed.

Sorry, Not Sorry

Overscheduling can increase stress, depression, and anxiety and cause burnout. This exercise gives you an opportunity to put the strategies just discussed into practice. Get ahead of any delegations of extra work by practicing saying no in a tactful way that allows you to set your boundaries and engage in a form of self-care.

Review the following scenario and write out what you could say in response. Practice saying no by reading your written script in the mirror or to people close to you.

While you are working on a time-sensitive task, your boss comes over and starts talking to you about a new project that needs to get done ASAP. You have an hour left before you need to submit the current task you are working on and are very focused on making sure you avoid errors. You reply to your boss's comments and continue to do your work. However, you realize you are off task, are forgetting the objectives for the task at hand, and are starting to feel very overwhelmed. Plus, you don't remember what your boss asked you to do because you were trying to concentrate on what you were already doing.

Write down what you could say or do to indicate to your boss that you are busy, without being rude or disrespectful. What do you think you could ask your boss to do to help you do your best work without getting distracted?

....

....

....

....

....

....

....

Diet and Nutrition

Healthy diet and nutrition practices can make a world of difference in treating ADHD symptoms by improving focus and attention, reducing hyperactivity, and promoting good moods and emotional regulation. Nutritional deficiencies, allergies, and even certain foods have been found to make some ADHD symptoms—such as inattention, hyperactivity, irritability, brain fog, and forgetfulness—worse. Food provides important building blocks for the body's various systems, including systems in the brain. Therefore, it's important to eat a healthy diet, consisting of high-protein, low-sugar, and low-carbohydrate foods; drink plenty of water; and eat lots of leafy green vegetables and fruits. It's never too late to invest in yourself by eating healthy. For breakfast, replace donuts or high-sugar cereals with a protein bar or steel-cut oatmeal with honey, bananas, or blueberries. For lunch, you can replace carbohydrate-rich sandwiches or pizza with avocado toast or a burrito bowl with brown rice instead of tortillas. Of course you can always speak with your doctor or a registered dietitian before making any changes to your diet. Consistently eating better on a daily basis by replacing foods at your own pace will lead to positive and lasting changes in the long term. Start small and keep working on improving your diet; if you end up making some unhealthy choices, that's okay—try to make a healthier choice at your next meal.

Some supplements are also helpful in managing overall brain and physical health. Turmeric and curcumin are natural herbs that help keep inflammation away; turmeric is also associated with having antibacterial properties, which can strengthen the immune system and increase its response to illness. Omega-3s with EPA, DHA, and GABA are found to protect the brain by slowing down the harmful impact of stress due to exposure to environmental toxins, excessive use of alcohol or drugs, and the normal aging process, as well as severe iron-deficiency anemia, which can cut off the healthy blood circulation—and oxygen—necessary for the brain's tissues to stay healthy. Certain supplements also boost production of "feel-good" neurotransmitters, or brain chemicals, such as dopamine and serotonin, and promote good moods.

A nutritionist or an integrative or functional medicine practitioner can help you learn more about healthy diet and the nutrition practices that lead to optimal brain health and functioning, helping you manage ADHD symptoms holistically, so you might consider setting up a consultation with one. In the meantime, here are some tips you can try out:

- **KEEP PROTEIN-RICH SNACKS ON HAND:** Use dried fruits, nuts, sunflower seeds, or protein bars as your go-to snack between meetings or classes. Almonds are great for boosting memory and providing the brain with the healthy fats it needs to function well. These foods are easy to eat quickly between meetings or during short walking breaks. Staying hydrated and eating small portions of food throughout the day can also prevent low blood sugar, which can cause irritability, shakiness, and inattentiveness.

- **TOSS OUT THE JUNK FOOD:** Avoid giving in to unhealthy cravings by stocking your shelves with healthy alternatives instead. Slowly switch out foods and reward yourself for your consistent efforts. You may feel "hangry" or irritable at first, but the change will become easier over time. Set reminders to take supplements as recommended by your health care provider.

- **PLAN AND PREP MEALS:** Prep meals for the week on Sundays by cooking a batch of healthy meals and storing them in containers. You can then take them with you for lunch or heat them up for dinner, thus limiting buying takeout.

Food and Mood Diary

A healthy diet and good nutrition can help improve overall brain function and decrease impulsivity, restlessness, and negative mood states, and increase concentration, attention, and emotional regulation. For this exercise, use the following chart to track what you are eating and how this food is impacting your mood and ADHD symptoms throughout the day. Ideally, try to stick with this diary for at least 30 days so you can notice any patterns or connections. If you can keep it going past 30 days, even better! Ultimately, if that seems overwhelming, start by committing to maintain this diary for at least five days. Use the insights you gain to make healthy changes to your diet and nutrition routine.

DAY 1

DATE: ....

MOOD: ....

BREAKFAST: ....

SNACKS: ....

DINNER: ....

MOOD: ....

ATTENTION: ....

IMPULSIVITY: ....

HYPERACTIVITY: ....

CONTINUED >

DAY 2

DATE: ....

MOOD: ....

BREAKFAST: ....

SNACKS: ....

DINNER: ....

MOOD: ....

ATTENTION: ....

IMPULSIVITY: ....

HYPERACTIVITY: ....

DAY 3

DATE: ....

MOOD: ....

BREAKFAST: ....

SNACKS: ....

DINNER: ....

MOOD: ....

ATTENTION: ....

IMPULSIVITY: ....

HYPERACTIVITY: ....

DAY 4

DATE: ....

MOOD: ....

BREAKFAST: ....

SNACKS: ....

DINNER: ....

MOOD: ....

ATTENTION: ....

IMPULSIVITY: ....

HYPERACTIVITY: ....

DAY 5

DATE: ....

MOOD: ....

BREAKFAST: ....

SNACKS: ....

DINNER: ....

MOOD: ....

ATTENTION: ....

IMPULSIVITY: ....

HYPERACTIVITY: ....

Sleep Habits

Sleep is a necessity, not a luxury, especially for the management of ADHD symptoms. Poor quality sleep or a lack of adequate amounts of sleep can lead to poor concentration, brain fog, emotional impulsivity, and temper outbursts. For instance, poor sleep can lead to road rage and a greater risk of car accidents due to emotionally explosive reactions to traffic or other drivers' actions. Not getting proper sleep on a regular basis also leads to an increase in anxiety and depression symptoms, further negatively impacting functioning at work and at home.

During sleep, your brain goes through a detoxing process where certain cells from your immune system act as vacuums, sucking up toxins that are present and promoting rest and increased brain capacity in the morning. The whole process is like pushing a reset button. This reset allows you to take on new information and process it without overwhelming your brain.

The circadian rhythm, or sleep cycle pattern, in humans is dependent on light; therefore, the body automatically prepares for sleep when natural light diminishes. Adults with ADHD may have impaired sleep cycles and are often referred to as night owls. As you may know already, it can be very challenging—if not impossible—to finally fall asleep at 3 or 5 a.m. and be at work by 7 a.m. You will miss early commitments, or go through the day with poor impulse control, poor attention, and emotional volatility. To combat the feelings of fatigue, many people use stimulants, such as nicotine and caffeine, to wake themselves up. Although these substances may increase alertness for a short time, they do not provide the alertness required to effectively engage executive functions to complete complicated tasks, manage impulsivity, and regulate other functions, such as hunger, blood sugar, mood, and hormone production. In fact, masking poor sleep by excessively consuming stimulants negatively impacts overall health and disrupts sleep even further by causing insomnia or sleep disorders.

There are a number of things you can do to help yourself get the sleep you need. Put your phone, tablet, and laptop away at least an hour before your targeted bedtime to prevent the blue light emitted by these devices from keeping your brain engaged and awake. You can try drinking hot, caffeine-free chamomile tea and other sleep-inducing teas that contain valerian root, an herb thought to promote sleep. Supplements like melatonin in dosages of 3 to 10 mg taken orally about two hours prior to your targeted bedtime may promote natural sleep onset and give you a more restful night's sleep. Of course, you should always consult your health care provider before starting any supplements or making changes to your treatment plan. Remember, the quality of your sleep tonight will determine the quality of your day tomorrow.

To achieve a healthy sleep pattern, try the following tips:

- Aim for seven to nine hours of sleep each night

- Read in bed to relax before turning out the light

- Keep the temperature in your bedroom cool

- Write down thoughts that keep you awake in a notebook next to your bed

- Use melatonin supplements (if approved by your health care provider) to induce natural sleep

- Avoid consuming alcohol or caffeine and doing exercise up to four hours before bedtime, or longer if you are taking stimulant medications for ADHD symptoms

- Focus on your breath, slow it down, and count backward from nine to zero, with each inhale and exhale becoming deeper and slower

Sleep Diary

Getting good sleep on a consistent basis is vital to managing ADHD symptoms effectively. Implement the strategies described in this section and use this sleep diary to track and monitor your sleep patterns.

DATE	HOURS SLEPT	TROUBLE SLEEPING?	POSSIBLE REASONS	MOOD NEXT DAY	ADHD-RELATED BEHAVIORAL SYMPTOMS PRESENT
		Y / N			
		Y / N			
		Y / N			
		Y / N			
		Y / N			
		Y / N			
		Y / N			
		Y / N			
		Y / N			
		Y / N			

Key Takeaways

The goal of this chapter was to strengthen your understanding of lifestyle changes you can make to manage your ADHD symptoms proactively and sustain the long-term, positive effects of ADHD treatment. Getting quality sleep, eating healthy foods, and managing daily stress levels are all lifestyle habits that facilitate a balanced and healthier mind and body—lowering the severity of ADHD symptoms and their impact on your personal and professional lives.

- Use the power of mindfulness and meditation exercises to develop a deeper self-awareness of the mind–body connection. Tune into your breath and focus on the sensations you notice as you inhale and exhale, with exhales being slightly longer. Or, while taking a shower, notice the sensation of the water on your skin, the smell of the soap, the sound of the water, and how the water droplets look as they fall. If you are short on time, tune into your breath and the sensory experience of the shower at the same time.

- Take an inventory of your dietary and nutritional habits. Go through your pantry and toss out junk food, candy, or foods filled with preservatives, and replace them with healthier, high-protein, high-fiber snacks that contain nuts and fruits. You can also stock up on protein bars with a high protein content and keep protein powder handy if you need to supplement your intake. Determine if you could benefit from taking multivitamins or additional supplements that contain zinc, omega-3s, magnesium, iron, and ginseng, for example. But remember to consult your health care provider prior to making any changes or using any supplements and herbs.

I will take care of my mind by taking care of my body.

The Road Forward

You have made it to the end of the workbook—congratulations! Through this workbook, you have learned to identify how ADHD may be impacting you in your personal and professional lives, while also looking at the nuances of adult ADHD, a diagnosis missed in the traditional diagnostic profile of a disorder thought to impact only children.

Chapters 1 and 2 focused on the various ways in which ADHD symptoms affect adults, including disinhibition, hyperactivity, distractibility, emotional dysregulation, and overall limitations on self-control due to impulsivity. Many adults with ADHD who were diagnosed later in life may have been predominantly inattentive as children, but they may not have displayed external behavior challenges and may have performed well enough academically to avoid teacher involvement. These chapters also emphasized that ADHD impairs the executive functioning skills responsible for engaging in the goal-directed behaviors needed to complete the essential tasks required of you at work or in your personal life. As a chronic neurodevelopmental disorder, ADHD is not curable, and symptoms impact all individuals differently. But there are many things you can do to manage ADHD and function as your best self.

As chapters 3 and 4 went on to cover, ADHD comes with traits found in highly successful people, such as creativity, passion for their work, intuition, and innovation. Embracing your neurodivergent presence in this world and using your strengths to do what you love and are good at are the keys to leading a successful and meaningful life.

Lastly, chapters 5 and 6 explored the ideas of getting professional help and personal support by having meaningful conversations with friends, family, coworkers, and managers to improve relationships and secure work accommodations that allow you to leverage your strengths and set you up for success. You also learned about the comprehensive treatment options available to you, including medication, behavior therapy, and lifestyle changes, as well as holistic strategies such as mindfulness and meditation practices, which promote positive coping skills and overall wellness for a happy, balanced, and more focused life.

All the chapters included ready-to-implement strategies, along with exercises to help you put what you learned into practice and easily transfer these changes into your daily life. You may feel a little overwhelmed by everything you have learned. Just remember to start with small actions, reward yourself for your efforts, embrace your strengths and your challenges, and most of all, accept yourself as the unique person you are.

Once again, congratulations for investing in yourself and completing this workbook. Although this workbook provided useful and practical information, remember that it is not meant to replace medical treatment or professional support. Be kind to yourself as you move forward on your ongoing journey to manage your ADHD symptoms. On challenging days, remind yourself that managing ADHD is a marathon, not a sprint, and you are doing the best you can. Finally, always keep in mind and be open to the wonderful possibilities that lie ahead.

RESOURCES

Websites

ADDITUDEMAG.COM A leading online resource owned by WebMD that offers numerous articles, virtual webinars, and e-books for professionals, parents of children with ADHD, and adults with ADHD. Its advisory board consists of research pioneers in the field, such as Dr. Hallowell and Dr. Barkley, among others.

ADD.ORG The Attention Deficit Disorder Association (ADDA) is an international nonprofit organization that aims to enrich the lives of adults with ADHD by sharing resources, support, and community programs. This organization has virtual support groups, a directory of ADHD professionals, and articles and other helpful information.

ADHDAWARENESSMONTH.ORG ADHD Awareness Month is held annually each October. It brings attention to a condition that is still misunderstood by many people. Each year has a theme. For example, "The Many Faces of ADHD" highlighted that ADHD affects all ages, genders, and social and economic groups. The month also celebrates the positive aspects of ADHD. Many health groups and government agencies get involved.

ASKJAN.ORG The Job Accommodations Network is a helpful resource for adults seeking information or support with requesting work accommodations.

CHADD.ORG Children and Adults with Attention-Deficit/Hyperactivity Disorder (CHADD) is a nonprofit organization founded to provide tools, support, and accommodations for adults and children alike with ADHD. This organization's website offers many valuable resources available to children and adults nationwide, including virtual support.

CDC.GOV/NCBDDD/ADHD The website for the Centers for Disease Control and Prevention (CDC) provides helpful information on ADHD, including diagnosis, treatment, and other supports available to children and adults, such as information regarding local processes and links to other helpful resources.

Books

The ADHD Effect on Marriage: Understand and Rebuild Your Relationship in Six Steps by Melissa Orlov
Untreated ADHD symptoms such as forgetfulness or impulsivity may cause conflict in marriages. This book addresses these patterns and offers six steps to rebuild a relationship.

The Mindfulness Prescription for Adult ADHD: An Eight-Step Program for Strengthening Attention, Managing Emotions, and Achieving Your Goals by Lidia Zylowska, MD
Mindfulness can help adults with ADHD improve focus and attention. In this book, Dr. Zylowska explains the benefits and how to practice mindfulness in your life.

Natural Relief for Adult ADHD: Complementary Strategies for Increasing Focus, Attention, and Motivation With or Without Medication by Stephanie Moulton Sarkis, PhD
People are usually very curious about whether ADHD can be treated naturally. In this book, the author offers a comprehensive overview of the different options, all backed by the latest research.

Taking Charge of Adult ADHD by Russell A. Barkley, PhD, with Christine M. Benton
This book, written by a leading authority in the field of ADHD, Dr. Russell Barkley, offers easy-to-follow information to address various areas of your life affected by ADHD, including information regarding medications and treatment options.

You can visit his website, RussellBarkley.org, to access more resources including links to ADHD videos.

Apps

FREEDOM An internet-blocking app you can customize to help you maintain healthy boundaries between work and home life, as well as minimize unproductive internet surfing.

INFLOW Founded by an ADHD coach, this app provides modules in different areas of an adult's life, such as work, parenting, home, and relationships, and provides short modules that offer more information and practice strategies.

TODOIST A popular app used to capture and organize tasks the moment they pop into your head, as well as set up reminders, organize and collaborate on tasks, prioritize projects and tasks, and monitor your productivity trends.

UNROLL.ME A free service that will clean up your email in-box, unsubscribe you from everything you don't want to receive, and get all the newsletters, listservs, and emails you want rolled into one daily digest. A hundred emails are turned into one email. Your in-box has never been happier.

REFERENCES

Amen, Daniel G. *Change Your Brain, Change Your Life: The Breakthrough Program for Conquering Anxiety, Depression, Obsessiveness, Lack of Focus, Anger, and Memory Problems.* New York: Harmony Books, 2015.

Barkley, Russell A., ed. *Attention-Deficit Hyperactivity Disorder: A Handbook for Diagnosis & Treatment.* 4th ed. New York: Guilford Press, 2015.

Barkley, Russell A., and Christine M. Benton. *Taking Charge of Adult ADHD.* New York: Guilford Press, 2010.

Brown, Thomas E. *Smart but Stuck: Emotions in Teens and Adults with ADHD.* San Francisco: Jossey-Bass, 2014.

Hallowell, Edward M., and John J. Ratey. *Delivered from Distraction: Getting the Most Out of Life with Attention Deficit Disorder.* New York: Ballantine Books, 2006.

Hallowell, Edward M., and John J. Ratey. *Driven to Distraction: Recognizing and Coping with Attention Deficit Disorder from Childhood through Adulthood.* New York: Anchor Books, 2011.

Linehan, Marsha M. *DBT Skills Training Handouts and Worksheets.* 2nd ed. New York: Guilford Press, 2015.

INDEX

About the Author

 **PUJA TRIVEDI PARIKH, LCSW, BCBA,** is a licensed psycho-therapist and behavior analyst with more than 12 years of clinical experience treating children and adults with ASD, ADHD, depression, and anxiety in various settings. She is the owner and founder of Pivotal Psychotherapy Services, P.C., where she provides research-based, integrative, and holistic interventions. Learn more about Puja's work at PivotalPsychotherapy.com.

Printed in the USA
CPSIA information can be obtained
at www.ICGtesting.com
CBHW050332310524
9306CB00009B/92